WALT
FRAZIER

Times BOOKS

WALT FRAZIER

One Magic Season and a Basketball Life

WALT FRAZIER
WITH NEIL OFFEN

Published in the United States by Times Books, a division of
Random House, Inc., New York, and simultaneously in
Canada by Random House of Canada Limited, Toronto.

Library of Congress Cataloging-in-Publication Data
Frazier, Walt, 1945–
Walt Frazier.
1. Frazier, Walt, 1945–   . 2. Basketball players—
United States—Biography. 3. New York Knickerbockers
(Basketball team) I. Offen, Neil. II. Title.
GV884.F7A3   1988   796.32′3′0924   [B]   88-40156
ISBN 0-8129-1736-7

Manufactured in the United States of America
9 8 7 6 5 4 3 2
First Edition

To my teammates, for making possible a season I'll never forget, and also to the thousands of Knicks fans who were teammates to us all.

Acknowledgments

Special thanks are due our editor, Jonathan Segal, whose idea this book was, and whose perseverance, insight, and great patience have brought it to fruition. We are also grateful to Sarah Van Tuyl and to the rest of the staff at Times Books, who immediately understood the idea of full-court pressure. We'd also like to thank for their assistance Bill Adler, Carol Offen, the sports information department at Southern Illinois University, and the New York Knicks' front office.

WALT FRAZIER

CHAPTER

1

IT WAS A CORNER HOTEL ROOM ON THE TWENTY-NINTH floor of the old New Yorker Hotel, overlooking Thirty-fourth Street and Eighth Avenue. There wasn't much there: a bed, a television, a small bathroom, and the largest clothing rack I could fit. This was my home. I stared at the clothing rack for a long time, wanting to pick out just the right outfit. Tonight, I told myself, I'm going to wear Clyde's best. For this game, I want to be in a special kind of mood. Dressed to a T.

It was late Friday afternoon, May 8, 1970, and tonight my team, the New York Knicks, was going to play the Los Angeles Lakers in game seven of the NBA finals. The winners would be the champions of pro basketball. The losers would be devastated. I heard on TV that it was a warm, sunny day, but I couldn't have told you that for sure; I couldn't tell much of anything from my small hotel window. Other than running out of the New Yorker for a morning practice across the street at Madison Square Garden, I'd stayed, snug and comfortable, in my own little world all day. I'd watched a little TV, some game shows and soap operas. I'd read the newspapers to find out if the reporters knew whether Willis Reed would play that night. I figured they knew more about it than I did.

The papers were filled with stories about the four students who had been killed at Kent State a few days before, and about the protests over it. There were articles about expanding the Vietnam War into Cambodia and about demonstrations calling for America to get out. But today I just couldn't concentrate on those things. All I cared about was Willis—and I couldn't find anything new about him, just the same reports that his chances of playing were fifty-fifty.

The only other time I'd left the hotel room was to go down to the hotel restaurant for lunch: steak and potatoes, cheese and toast. I ate alone. I like to eat alone. In the papers and on TV, I was flashy Clyde, the well-dressed man about town. But I was often reclusive during the season, particularly when I had some thinking and preparing to do. I ate a little earlier than I normally did, because I wanted to be hungry when I got out on the court. I didn't want to feel bogged down with food. Tonight I wanted a real empty feeling in my stomach. I wanted to feel that I could fly.

After lunch, I took the elevator back upstairs and pushed my half of the plug into the keyhole. I didn't keep much stuff in my room, but I was always worried about getting ripped off, so I used this device called a plug, sort of half a molded lock, inserted into the door. The door would only open if you had the matching half, which meant that no one else could put a key in the lock. The maids were always upset with me because they couldn't get in my room to clean or make the bed.

I lay back down on the bed and rested. I suppose it was my only real superstition as a player. One time in high school, in the tenth grade, I walked my girlfriend home before a crucial game. She lived three or four miles from my house in Atlanta, and I went all the way out there and back. I was exhausted that night; my legs felt like they had bricks attached to them, and I played an atrocious game. My school, Howard High, lost. From that time on, I told myself I would always be prepared to play. On the day of a game, I didn't do much of anything, trying to conserve my energy. I would just lie around, stay off my feet, and store up my juice for the game.

I tried to take a nap, but it wouldn't come. Finally, I got up and started looking at the clothes rack. I fingered the sleeves of a couple of suits. What I wear exemplifies the way I feel, and I wanted to feel especially up and good about myself that night. I needed to wear something bright and positive. From the forty outfits I had at that time I chose a sharp black-and-white plaid suit with a gray background. From my thirty pairs of shoes, I settled on the black-and-white lizard skins. I tied a black ascot around my neck. I spent more than my usual time—and even my usual time was a lot—fixing my hair. I was going to have a good time tonight. It would be time to party. I was determined to be Clyde tonight.

It was Danny Whelan, the Knicks' trainer, who first called me Clyde. Whenever we were on the road, whatever city I was in, I would always go out and look around at clothes in the shops. One time when we were in Baltimore, I had seen a brown velour Borsalino hat that just knocked me out. I paid around eighty dollars for the hat, which in those days was a lot of bucks. The first time I wore it, the other guys on the team laughed at me. We were outside the Baltimore Civic Center, waiting for the bus, and Dick Barnett was getting on me, saying, "Hey, man, where'd you get that thing? You been buyin' at Goodwill again?" The Bullets were there, too, and they kept staring at me with funny looks on their faces. The thing was, the hat had a wide brim, not a narrow one, and nobody was wearing that kind back then. I had been insecure about putting it on at first, but after a while, when all the guys finally stopped laughing, I thought, To hell with them. Hey, man, I'm going to wear it. I'll wear what I think looks good on me. A little bit after that, the movie *Bonnie and Clyde* came out, and one night in the locker room when I was wearing the Borsalino, Danny said, "Hey, look at Clyde over there," and that's how it stuck.

But Clyde was more than just a dude wearing a flashy hat. Over the course of a couple of years with the Knicks, Clyde developed into a whole personality. Clyde became the guy who liked the limelight. Clyde liked to go out dancing and hit the clubs. Clyde was showtime, but Clyde was only half of my personality. If Clyde liked the limelight, Walt was the shy young man I had always been, the one I had been brought up to be. Though Clyde hit the clubs at night, Walt went to bed early and alone. Clyde was the fun-lover who went out, but only after we had played a good game (and *I* had played a good game). If we lost, Walt would go home quietly, because there was no joy in having a good time after we had lost a game. I felt I didn't deserve to be Clyde then; I had to stay home and sacrifice and be Walt.

Walt was the person I had always been, growing up in Atlanta, at college in Illinois, even when I first came to the Knicks. He was a guy under control, not too comfortable with other people, careful never to go where he didn't belong, and usually needing no one but himself to get through the day. As my ballplaying and the Knicks improved, and as I got more comfortable with living in New York City, I started to lose some of my shyness. A new part of me started to emerge: Clyde. If Walt was still shy, at least some of the time, particularly when people fussed over him, Clyde was a great cover for Walt's shyness. Clyde and Walt were like two parts of the same person, two personalities within the same body.

I could choose who I wanted to be, like selecting a suit I wanted to wear. I showed Clyde to the world and kept Walt to myself. It was a good balance.

I crossed Eighth Avenue to the Garden, and the sidewalk was lined with people: a lot of regulars, but a lot of new faces, too. "Clyde, you got it tonight! You got it tonight!" somebody screamed at me as I went inside the players' entrance on Thirty-third Street. I took the elevator to the fifth floor and the operator told me, "Don't forget, this is the big one tonight." Like I could forget.

I got to the Knicks' locker room exactly one hour before game time, the minimum arrival time, the last guy to show up. Everyone else seemed to have been there for a long time. Most of the guys were already dressed. For the first time, the significance of what was going on hit me. I asked nobody in particular if Willis was there. Somebody said, "Yeah," and nodded toward the trainer's room. I went in to see if I could find out more than the newspapers had told me. All *they* had said was that nothing was sure.

Willis was leaning on the training table, looking down at

his legs. "Hey, man. What is it? Are you in or not?" I asked him.

Reed answered slowly, "I don't know. Really don't know. I might, and I might not."

I figured that meant no. Normally, I was full of confidence, but when I heard Willis say that, I began to feel apprehensive. Willis was our main man, our number-one scorer and rebounder, our captain—and how were we going to throw Nate Bowman, our Psychedelic Sid, against Wilt Chamberlain? I said to myself, Well, if we don't win it, I think I can live with that. Winning the championship was never my ultimate goal, the prize I always chased after. Just getting to play in the NBA, just being able to stay there, was more than I'd ever expected. That was enough. Anything else would be gravy. I thought, If we don't get it this year, I can wait—we'll probably be back again. I was young, twenty-five years old, and I guess not all that smart—I didn't even realize how far I'd come.

CHAPTER
2

O N THE OUTSKIRTS OF NOWHERE, WHAT SEEMED about a thousand miles from civilization, was the State University of New York in Farmingdale, Long Island. Farmingdale was just like the name implied: "Farmer in the Dell," we used to call it. "There are *cows* around here," I'd tell friends from the city. It was a great place to do nothing. On September 15, 1969, the Knicks opened their preseason training camp there.

Two days earlier, I had read in the papers that John Warren, the Knicks' number-one draft choice, had signed a guaranteed three-year contract for $100,000. That was real money. The ABA was in business then, and the Nets, the other local pro team, had also wanted him. Nobody resented the contract; the rest of us just resented not having the chance to make that much ourselves.

I was making $25,000 a year, and the season before I had set a team-assist record and been named to the NBA all-defensive team. I was going into the third year of my three-year contract and a couple of months earlier I had asked Red Holzman, the coach, for a raise. I didn't have an agent, so I just went in to see him myself. I told him I wanted at least $100,000 for the next three years, maybe $125,000 or even $150,000. "Sorry, Clyde," he told me. "No way. You got another year on your contract." That was it and I was definitely not happy, but I didn't say anything at the time.

When camp started, I hadn't touched a basketball for four months, since we had lost to the Celtics in the Eastern Division finals the season before. I didn't want to touch one. My strategy was that I wanted to really miss the game: I wanted to miss shooting the ball, the feeling of it rolling off my fingers. And then, all of a sudden, I would find myself anxious and ready to go, wanting to touch a ball and play again.

I also hadn't seen any of the guys on the team over the summer. I was always surprised when people would ask me, "Hey, have you talked to Barnett?" "How's Cazzie doing?" I had no idea. It was the same kind of thing as not touching a basketball. After spending nine months of the year living with the same guys, seeing them every day, you get a little tired of them. When you work with people every day, you don't necessarily communicate with them during your time off.

I drove up from Atlanta, got lost as usual coming out of the Lincoln Tunnel, and drove out to Farmingdale. This time I was glad to see all the guys.

In training camp, after three months away, *everyone* is usually happy to see everyone else, and the camaraderie is good. This camp was a comfortable one where everyone felt he belonged. Except for Phil Jackson, who had a back problem, all the players were returning from the Knick team that had come on strong and finished third in the East the previous season. We were adding Warren and Dave Stallworth, who was trying to come back from what everyone thought was a heart attack. And no one was going to win a job—or lose one—in this training camp. There were twelve spots on the roster and eleven veterans with signed contracts, plus Warren, to fill them. There wasn't any fear among the players that if you screwed up, you were gone. Instead, this was a camp to sharpen our skills and get us ready for the long season ahead of us.

The mood was very up. I heard it first from Willis. We were getting dressed after one of Red's killer morning defense workouts. Reed was the captain, and he always had a positive attitude. I think he felt it was his responsibility to motivate the rest of the players. "You know, man," he was saying as he sort of shook his head, like he didn't completely believe it himself, "we can take it this year. Damn it, we can."

I guess it was pretty obvious. Ever since the Knicks had traded Walt Bellamy and Howie Komives to Detroit for Dave DeBusschere the year before, things had really started to come together. After Dave arrived, we had won three out of every four games, and there was a real sense that the puzzle was complete. This season, we'd have Dave from the beginning and the Celtics wouldn't have Bill Russell anymore. There was a hopeful feeling in camp that you just couldn't escape.

It wasn't the players so much who were talking us up. There were a lot of reporters around the camp—more than usual, it seemed—who kept telling us that we should finish first, that they *expected* it of us. The fans seemed to be up, too. Guys would drive out from the city to watch us, even though the practices were closed. Even management was up, and the Garden executive types at Farmingdale were always smiling and joking. The excitement began to filter through to the players, even though we didn't talk about it very much.

Red Holzman never said a word about the high expectations. That wasn't his way. Red is always very business-like—low-key and calm. He never called the team together during camp to talk about the upcoming season. He just went about his job of preparing us without any crap.

Red was named coach of the Knicks in the middle of the 1967–68 season, my rookie year. He came to a terrible team, where no one passed the ball and no one played defense. Guys like Komives and Bellamy were unbelievably selfish. Under Dick McGuire, who had been the coach before Red, everybody went his own way. Dick was very lenient with the players, and they took advantage of it. Before a game, the Knicks' locker room was like a circus. Whenever I walked in, I could hardly get past all the hangers-on so I could get dressed. There were people in there getting autographs and guys making business deals. I thought one guy I saw there all the time was one of the owners of the team, but it turned out he was just a friend of a friend of somebody.

The first day Red was coach, he said, "There'll be no more of this stuff. The locker room is for the players." The day after he was appointed, Red called a meeting for ten-thirty in the morning. Bill Bradley was a couple of minutes late. Bradley had just signed a huge contract, but Red bawled him out and fined him right on the spot. Hey, man, if he could do that to Bill Bradley, he could do it to *anybody*. We knew Red was serious. He gained our respect right away.

Red even went after Willis. Soon after the coaching change, we were playing Cincinnati and Willis was having a bad game. Red took him out, and Willis was mad. He didn't say a word and went to sit at the far end of the bench. Red waited until Willis sat down and then said, "Willis, get your ass over here and sit right by me." He was telling him, "Don't get angry and go to the end." Red made Willis sit next to him and then he told Willis point by point what he was doing wrong.

Dick McGuire had been too nice a guy to be a coach. If he fined you today, you could come to him tomorrow, say you were a little low on funds, and talk him out of it. Dick believed that pro players would do what they should do. And that was his problem. Guys had even been eating hot dogs at halftime. Red cut that out, and a lot of other things, too. Red said, "No more signing autographs before the game. No more being late for meetings." Under Dick, we rarely worked out on off-days, but Red put in two-a-day practices. He made us play full-court defense—pressing and trapping, picking up our man from the time the ball was passed in, from end line to end line.

A lot of guys weren't too happy about this new regime. In the locker room, Komives—who was still with us when Red took over—grumbled, "Hey, man, what kind of bullshit is this?" And Dick Barnett answered, "Yeah, man, you know it."

On the other hand, I loved it. I liked discipline. I wanted it. With McGuire, there hadn't been any, and I was floundering. I loved defense, and Red was above all a defensive coach. On offense, for the most part, we put in our own plays, plays DeBusschere had brought with him from Detroit, or plays that we ripped off of the Celtics, Golden State, or other teams. Red concentrated on defense, always trying to get us to focus on getting back, seeing the ball, knowing where our man was at all times, *seeing the ball.*

All through my basketball career, my coaches had been disciplinarians. You did it their way. "His way or the highway," we used to say. I had known Red a little when he was the team's chief scout. He always kidded around with me then, never saying anything serious. But when he became the coach, hey, the kidding stopped. At the first meeting, he threatened us. "If you guys make my life miserable, I'm going to make your life miserable," he warned. "There'll be extra practice. You'll have to watch films until you go blind." In a very low voice, Red told us, "I want a team. No more selfish crap. You guys have got to play together. And the guys who don't play that way won't play." Red also threatened that if we didn't play his way, he would make us do all the things that pro players don't want to do because they take up your whole day.

Unlike Dick, Red understood the players' psychology. He knew that most of us would do something only if we were forced to do it. But Red was fair. Win or lose, he talked to you. He let you know what was on his mind. For him, there was only one set of rules, and everybody had to follow it. Still, Red understood each player and the player's needs, what that player needed to do, how he could function in a team concept. Red knew he could talk to me, yell at me, and it wouldn't bother me. Sometimes, even when I was sitting

near him on the bench, he'd call my name as if I were playing and say, "Clyde! Clyde! Get up on him!" I was his whipping boy. It was always "Get up on your man, Clyde. . . . "
"Clyde, do this. . . ." "Clyde, do that. . . . " He knew it was
like talking to a wall. But Red also knew he couldn't yell too
much at Bradley, because Bill would only play worse. While
he kicked my butt, Red would pat Bradley on his.

Even though I was his whipping boy, I was also Red's
pet. His key man, he called me. Every hotel we'd go into,
Red would put all the room keys in my pocket and say,
"Clyde, you're my key man."

I owe my success to Red, and I'll never forget that. My
rookie year was tough. With an ankle injury and without any
discipline, I wasn't playing the way I knew I could, and I was
down. I wasn't even starting—or getting too many minutes
of playing time—on what was a really dreadful team. I was
still playing badly a few games after Red took over. We were
coming back from Philadelphia on the bus after another
loss. A couple of the guys were up front, playing cards.
Before we got on the bus, Red told me he wanted to talk to
me on the way back, so I had to sit next to him.

"I scouted you in college," he said. "I know you're a
much better player than what you're showing. So what's
your problem?"

"I don't know. Wish I did."

"You got talent. You got real ability that you're not

showing. You just gotta get out there and stop playing scared. You gotta play the way I saw you play in college."

He also told me he liked my defense and because of that he was going to give me more playing time. I could feel the confidence flowing right into my body.

Seventeen years later, in Springfield, Massachusetts, Red presented me with my plaque when I was inducted into the Basketball Hall of Fame. A guy said a few words into the mike, and then Red just smiled and handed it over. And I thought, Justice is done. If it hadn't been for Red, I wouldn't have had a Hall of Fame career.

The media that year always talked about Knick chemistry, how all the pieces fit together just right. The chemistry was Red Holzman. All the pieces of the puzzle were there after DeBusschere arrived. But Red put those pieces together.

Red's morning workouts were designed to get us into game condition. Although I hadn't touched a ball all summer, I came to camp in reasonable shape. I had done some weightlifting and had started my running about two weeks earlier than usual. The year before, Red's first camp as coach, I hadn't really prepared myself. I didn't think it would be necessary. I assumed that I could get ready in just a couple of weeks, and only started to work out right before the beginning of camp. When Red had us play full court, one-on-one, that year, I felt my heart fluttering from the exertion. The pain was excruciating. I didn't want to go through that again.

The guards, the smaller guys like me, were usually ready when camp opened. The big people, like Willis and Dave, were in terrible shape when they arrived. They were lazy, and preferred to play themselves into condition. Dave really dreaded camp, yet he would never prepare himself so it wouldn't be such torture for him. The worst, though, when it came to preseason preparation, was Walt Bellamy. When he was with the Knicks, he always tried to hold out until training camp was almost over, and then he would sign his contract just before the season started. One time, at the end of a camp practice, Bells, who was 6′ 11″ and liked his pancakes and waffles for breakfast, leaned on the wall outside the showers. That was as far as he got. I went in and took my shower. When I came out, Bells was still in the same position. He may still be there.

Red had his killer drills to whip us into shape. He would roll a ball down to the end of the court. You had to go get it before it went out of bounds, dribble it to the other end and score, and then dribble down the court and score at the other end. Fast, faster, faster. The morning session always ended with the suicide drills: the final torture. You start running at one end line and then go to the free-throw line nearest to you and then back to the end line. Then, without stopping, you run to center court and back again to the end line. Then to the far free-throw line and back to the end line. Finally, all the way to the other end line and back. That was one suicide drill, and you had to do it by time. You had to do it all in thirty or thirty-five seconds, nothing slower. We did it by teams, blue jerseys against red jerseys. If you saw that one of the big guys—Reed, DeBusschere, or Nate Bowman—was on your team, you tried turning your shirt around to change colors, because the slower team got the prize of doing one more suicide drill.

Red devoted these morning sessions to fundamentals—passing, dribbling, shooting, positioning: the basics. You'd go up and down the court dribbling and passing and then positioning yourself against the guys coming down the other way. The guards always had to pick up their man from end line to end line. There were chase drills where I'd start two steps in front of my man, who would have to run and catch me and try to block my shot if he could. Then it would be my turn to try it on him. Whether I made the shot or missed it, the defender had to get the rebound and come back the other way with me chasing him. Then we'd have two-on-two, full court, a guard and a forward racing up and back. And always with Red screaming, "Get up! See the ball, Clyde! Come on, move it! Willis, get up! See the ball, see your man, Clyde! Move, Bradley, move!"

The first couple of days, my feet hurt so much I slept

with them up on the wall. My body ached all over. I've seen men cry during training camp, and I've seen guys throwing up *and* crying. In those early days, there were a few rookie free agents in camp, and during one morning drill one of them just ran out of the gym and disappeared.

The morning drills lasted from 11:00 A.M. to 1:00 P.M., when we broke for lunch. The team didn't have to eat lunch together, so most of the guys would just go off on their own. Unfortunately, there weren't a lot of places to go to in Farmingdale. Most of us headed back to where we were staying, sort of a poor man's Holiday Inn about a ten-minute drive from the gym. They had an all-you-could-eat deal for around three dollars. Problem was, it was overpriced.

We had to be back in the gym by five, which sounds like a lot of time but really wasn't. After we had showered, it was already two o'clock. By the time we ate, it was three-thirty. By the time you'd fall asleep—if you could—it was quarter past four.

Evening practices, which also lasted two hours, began at five. This was the time to go over the plays, work on game situations, dummy in the things we would actually be using during the season. Out of about twenty-five plays, five worked. One of the main ones we practiced was called "Barry," or sometimes "Golden State." DeBusschere or Bradley would be on the weak side. I'd dribble toward him and he would fake that he was clearing out the area. Then he'd cross into the lane and come back to me, and I would shield his man with my body and hand him the ball on the baseline. Jump shot. We worked on what we called the "fist play." I'd raise my fist, and Barnett would try to rub his man off on Dave's pick, and I'd get the ball to him. If DeBusschere's man switched, then Dave would go backdoor.

After the plays, we'd start the practice games. Red always arranged to have some quick guard in camp whom I'd have to cover, to make sure I would really be in shape. Milt Williams was this camp's designated rabbit. He was a quiet guy from a small college in the Midwest, and he could play. He was quick and could penetrate and then dish off, but we all knew there was no way he was going to make the team.

I felt that either Donnie May or Bill Hosket should have been cut, and Williams should have stayed. May and Hosket were the last two guys on the bench and only got into a game if it was a real blowout. But they ended up making the team because they had guaranteed contracts. They were top draft picks, and how could the Knicks just get rid of them? We're talking about corporate ego here—and money. And it didn't hurt that they were white. The unstated "rule" in the NBA at the time was basically that if you were black, you were playing. Not too many black guys were sitting on the bench. I think of all the blacks playing in the league then, probably over 50 percent of them were starters. It was understood and accepted throughout the NBA that teams could only have so many blacks on their squads. The ratio was supposed to be about 60 percent white to 40 percent black. If talent had been the only consideration, it probably should have been 60 percent black and 40 percent white. Milt Williams was probably the second-best guard in camp; he had out-played Mike Riordan and even Dick Barnett. But Milt got caught up in the numbers game. Or Red saw some things I hadn't.

At 7:00 P.M. we were finally done—and that was the word for it. After showering, Reed, DeBusschere, and Riordan headed off to a nearby tavern to have a few beers. They always liked to relax a bit before we met in the campus cafeteria for dinner. Then it was 9:00 P.M., and we were free for whatever we wanted to do. Of course, it was late already and we were out in Farmingdale, which was exactly Red's strategy.

For the first two or three days, it worked. I looked out my motel window and saw everyone's car in the parking lot at 10:00 P.M. A day or two later, some cars were gone. By the fourth or fifth day, almost all the cars were gone by 11:00 P.M. The guys were confident. They were getting into shape and knew they could now take off for the pleasures of the city. By then, the monotony of camp had set in. We were all bored. That kind of boredom drives players to retire. If they could skip training camp, I'm sure a lot of guys would play longer.

After ten boring days, we were finally able to start playing preseason games. Preseason games were sort of like going to a dance with your sister. You do most of the same steps, but it just doesn't mean the same thing. Barnett was always saying about them, "They are not *ree-yull*"—but at least they were better and a little more interesting than camp. At Farmingdale after a while, guys got to know your every move since they played you every day and it got difficult to fake them out. With exhibition games, at least you could try to fake someone else out. You had more of a chance, anyway.

We headed out to Roanoke, Virginia, and Saginaw, Michigan, and Utica, New York, where we beat the defending-champion Celtics. They were playing for the first time in over a decade without Bill Russell, who had retired over the summer. Instead of Russell, they had somebody named Henry Finkel in the middle. It wasn't exactly the same as playing against Russell. Even though we won, somebody stole the headline in the local newspaper by jumping out of a window. It was a bigger story than a victory by the Knicks, and like typical ballplayers concerned only with what we were doing, we couldn't figure out why that had pushed us off the front of the paper.

Just before the preseason ended, Milt Williams was cut. I wasn't surprised. And a couple of days before we broke camp, Red called me into his office. He had seen, he told me, that I was still hustling. I wasn't dogging it, and I wasn't sulking about not getting the extra money I wanted. He said he would go to management and tell them to give me the new contract I had been asking for.

"That's all right, Red," I told him. "I'll just play out the old one and see how it goes."

CHAPTER
3

FINALLY, THE GAMES WERE FOR *REE-YULL*. WE OPENED against Seattle at Madison Square Garden, in front of a full house of Knick fans. This was the new Garden, our first full season there, and I still missed the old place up on Fiftieth Street. I had come to New York for the first time when I was in college at Southern Illinois University to play in the NIT Tournament at the old Garden. It was a disappointment when I saw the place for the first time. I had heard about it for so long, since I was a kid, and what I saw finally was just a large, dilapidated building in a pretty dreary area. It was a dump. I suppose I had looked at the old Garden with big eyes, just what you'd expect from a young, shy black kid from the South who had lived a pretty sheltered life.

Growing up in Atlanta, I was the oldest of nine kids— seven sisters who came after me, and then my brother. There were fourteen years from me to my brother, and as the oldest, I took care of the others, chastising them and cooking for them. I changed diapers and burped babies and I sewed and scrubbed the floors and washed the other kids. I was always aware that they followed me and looked up to me. I was their parent when my mother wasn't around.

That was partly because my father, Walt Senior, wasn't around very much. At first, he had always been out "working." My father was a hustler. I guess he was in the numbers racket, but I never really knew exactly. All I did know was that he always had lots of fancy clothes and sometimes money to throw around, and there were always people coming over and hanging around the house. If I needed a ride somewhere, there was always one of his people to take me there in a fancy car.

My father was a big, handsome man, a sharp dresser, and when he wasn't home, I'd put on his shoes and shirts, even though they were all much too large for me. I couldn't wait till I got big enough to wear his watches and his rings.

Everybody played the numbers, and my father controlled a part of it. But when I was around ten or eleven years old, something must have happened in the numbers rackets, and then he must have lost his territory. I never asked him exactly what had happened. Maybe I didn't want to know. But from then on, there was a lot less money. We no longer had a maid coming once a week to clean the house. Suddenly, there were no more people hanging around in the living room, and no more expensive cars. It was like everyone had just disappeared.

Afterward, my father sort of broke down. He started to drift and wasn't around very much anymore. Although he left his clothes in the closet, he came home sporadically if at all. He didn't work and didn't seem to care much about anything. He'd hang out mostly down by the pool hall on Auburn Avenue. When I'd ask my mom for some money, she'd say, "Go down to the street and ask your father." I would, and he'd always give me something. If the Globetrotters were in town and I needed tickets to the game, somehow he would get them for me. I don't know how he did it, but he always came through. He'd get me two tickets, but would never be interested or have enough time or whatever to come with me himself. He'd suggest I get somebody else to go with me. Sometimes, when I needed a car to drive and there was no one else to turn to, he'd get me one, even though I didn't have a driver's license yet. But he'd never drive me himself.

Ever since that time, my father has continued to drift along. I'm not exactly sure how he survives. I guess he works when he needs to. My sister Mary keeps an eye on him and says he's doing all right. I keep in touch with him at a distance, a phone call around the holidays. I suppose I've drifted away, too, but I still love him. He's still my father.

As I got older, I didn't ask my father for much, or my mom for many things, either. From about the age of thirteen on, I made a point of never asking her for money or anything she couldn't afford because of all her kids. If I wanted something, I would use my own money. I always had jobs. In the summer, I'd cut grass. I'd go to white areas of Atlanta with my best friend, and if the lawns seemed to need a trim, we'd knock on the doors. We could make almost twenty dollars apiece for a day's work. I worked construction jobs and as a busboy, I cleaned carpets and trucked cotton.

If I really needed something and didn't have the money, my uncle Eddie took care of me. Eddie Wynn was my mother's brother, and only about eight years older than I was. When I was seven or eight, he was the guy I used to hang around with and tag after. He would take me around to the playgrounds and brag to the guys what a great athlete I was going to be. He was a trainer for his high school team, and I used to go to all the games on the bus with him. He would get all the old sneakers from the team and would find my size and give them to me when I needed sneakers. When I needed special clothes for the high school prom, it was Uncle Eddie who took care of it. When he was working for a dry cleaner after vocational school, and I was still in high school, he would lend me his car if he didn't need it. If I was the big brother to the other kids, Uncle Eddie was *my* big brother.

With Uncle Eddie, and my grandparents and my mother to take care of me, I wasn't bitter that my father wasn't there. That was just the way it was.

Even after what happened to my father, we still weren't poor. We all slept in separate beds. Mine was a hideaway bed in our part of the duplex house we shared with my grandparents. When my mother was away from the house, my father's parents were there to look after us. After years of working at the Atlanta Paper Company, my grandfather had retired, but he never took it easy. He couldn't stop fiddling around the house, working in the yard—always working at something. He wanted everybody else to be doing something, too. I'd by lying in bed on Saturday morning, exhausted after a tough Friday night football game, and my grandfather would come over and start shaking me awake so I'd go out and cut the grass. "Later, later," I'd say. "Leave me alone. Go away." My grandmother was a part-time domestic, working for the white folks in the better neighborhoods of Atlanta. From time to time, they would give her things. As a kid growing up, my best clothes—not the most fashionable, but the ones in the best condition—were the hand-me-downs white people had given away to my grandmother.

We'd have some meals in my parents' part of the duplex, and some meals over in my grandparents' part. The best meals were the Sunday breakfasts, which weren't really breakfasts at all, but could fill you up for the whole day. For once, the whole family would be there, and my grandmother would bring out biscuits and chicken and whatever else she had around. Grandma would spend the entire meal forcing more and more food on me and telling me to eat this and try some more of that. All the time, Grandpa would be saying to her, "Don't beg him to eat. Beg him *not* to eat."

We always had enough food. We couldn't go shopping every day, but once a week we could get what we needed. We had clothes that were clean and we dressed neatly. My mother wasn't like my father—she didn't know anything about fashion, and didn't care about it at all—but she'd always tell us how important it was to be neat.

We lived in a lower-class neighborhood, but we were a lot better off than the families who lived in the projects. It was an all-black neighborhood, and the only white people I saw owned the grocery stores. During the summer, I'd play football against white kids in pickup games, but when we got to be around nine or ten years old, the white kids wouldn't or couldn't play with us anymore. Their parents would tell them, "Don't play with the niggers."

In the early 1950s, Deep South segregation was still the rule in Atlanta. When I got on the bus, I knew I had to go to the back, so that's where I went. I remember going to the rear of restaurants to get food, because we weren't allowed to go to the front. But I didn't know anything else, so I accepted it. I was the type of kid who never wanted to go anyplace I wasn't wanted. So I never had any problems with white people. When the guys wanted to go to a place or an area we all knew we shouldn't go to, they'd go anyway. I'd go home. Yeah, there were a few times kids called me nigger. A car would ride by as I was walking home at night after a ballgame, and someone would shout out, "Hey, nigger, get off the streets." My grandfather, though, had always told me, "A man is a man." I'd let it go, and for the most part, I was never in too many places where anyone had a chance to call me nigger.

I didn't know I was supposed to be unhappy or feel deprived. I thought I was having a terrific time, going to the ballpark where the Southern Association Atlanta Crackers played and where my friends and I would get in free because we cleaned up the park. We got the players' broken bats. When they hit home runs, we used to go behind the outfield signs and get the balls. We'd stand under the bleachers and give people in the stands hotfoots. When we played basketball on a dirt court at the playground a few blocks from my house, I thought it was heaven, as long as it didn't rain.

Maybe because Southern Illinois won the NIT and I won the MVP, I fell in love with the old Madison Square Garden. There was a mystique about it. The people were right on top of you, and you could almost feel their breathing. They never stopped screaming and shouting the whole game. These fans were crazy, and I hoped I could play in New York, in front of people like that. I had never seen fans react that way about basketball before. During my rookie year, we had a noon game against Philadelphia, and as I walked out onto the court, I said to myself, Who in the hell is going to come to a game at noon? Only around nineteen thousand people. The place was mobbed with kids. I couldn't believe it. "This is incredible," I said to Barnett. "This is New York City, man," he told me.

At the new Garden, the people were too far away. You couldn't hear their words or feel their presence in quite the same way.

Then again, the fans couldn't throw paper onto the floor at you, either. In the old Garden, the locker room had been huge. The ceiling was so high it made you feel tiny. The showers all seemed to be set up for Wilt Chamberlain, the heads so high that they sprayed water all over and you felt you could drown. The new Garden was shiny and slick, but I think they spent all the money on the outside. The players didn't have anything. The locker rooms were very small, and when we first moved in, we didn't even have cubicles for our stuff. There wasn't even a place for me to hang my mink coat! We finally got cubby holes and small, individual stalls with a trunk to put our personal belongings in.

The opening game of the 1969 season began just like any other game. Before we went on the floor, Red gave his usual speech: Clyde, you know who you're guarding. Willis, remember who you're on . . . and so on and so on. He didn't make any big thing about starting off the year or about the high expectations everybody had for us. He read the scouting report. They were running a lot; on defense they looked to trap a lot on the baseline.

We lined up at center court as John Condon, the public-address announcer, introduced us individually. The fans were screaming for every name. They loved DeBusschere, were crazy about Willis. But when Dave Stallworth's name was announced, they stood and gave him an ovation. Stalls ran out and shook hands, but he had sort of a far-off look in his eyes. He wasn't really looking at us. I think he wished he were somewhere else.

The Rave had missed the last two seasons with what everybody—including Stalls himself, at first—thought was a heart attack. It turned out to be something like an infection in the wall of his heart, he explained to us. But if he was being allowed to come back and play, we all figured the doctors had probably diagnosed it wrong. Of course, if you knew the Rave, you'd understand why it *could* have been a heart attack. Dave was a very high-strung person, a perpetual-motion man. He always liked to have his tape player going, and even when he was walking, he seemed to be dancing to the beat. With Cazzie and Bowman, who had been his college roommate at Wichita State, he'd zip out of the locker room to go party. They were always interested in the ladies. "Let us have us a time," the Rave would say.

The same year the Knicks took Bradley as a first-round draft choice, they had another first-round pick, and they took Stalls with that one. A 6′ 7″ all-American at Wichita State, he could really do it all. I had to guard him once in college when I was a sophomore at Southern Illinois. One time he came out on the floor and was playing center; the next time, he's a forward. Another time, he comes out and plays a guard, bringing the ball up. I never knew where to find him. Even at his height, he could handle the ball, run the floor, and still get up on the boards. If he came out of college today, he'd be a big guard, in the Magic Johnson mold.

Although he had unlimited potential, I don't think the Rave ever really fulfilled it. Part of the reason, of course, was the heart problem, and the two seasons he missed. Even though he started working out about eight months after the "attack," when he saw he could handle it physically, it was still pretty tough for him to miss so much time playing at the highest level of competition.

But I also think that Stalls liked his good times maybe a little too much. He had so much natural ability, the game came so easily to him, that I felt Stalls never dedicated himself to improving those skills. A few years later, when the

Knicks traded Stallworth and Mike Riordan to the Bullets for Earl Monroe, it was Dave who Baltimore coach Gene Shue really wanted. He was going to be the starter, but that turned out to be Riordan, and Stallworth was on the bench once again, still sitting with unfulfilled potential.

In camp, no one had taken it easy on Stallworth. "Hey, you got some tape or something over your heart?" Barnett asked him. Everybody was trying to solidify his own job, work himself into shape, and nobody had any time for sympathy. But Red and Danny handled the Rave with kid gloves. Red took it easy on him by putting Stalls in at first for only five minutes at a time. Danny monitored his health very closely. The rest of us forgot about his heart until we played that exhibition game against the Celtics. The Rave went up on the offensive boards, got banged by one of the Celtics, and went down on the floor. Everyone held his breath, including the crowd. I was halfway downcourt and turned and stared. Slowly, the Rave got up, with a big smile on his face. From that moment on, I think we all felt he was okay, and would be fine for the entire season.

With the fans screaming, we blew by the Supersonics on opening night. The next night in Cincinnati it was a tight game near the end of the third quarter when Cazzie Russell came in off the bench. We immediately called his play. Willis and Barnett set a double pick down low for him, Cazzie came off it, I got him the ball, he shot and scored. Once he hit the first one, you could feel he was going to get on a roll. He hit another from the corner, his favorite spot, one from the top of the key, and put together nine straight points as we blew the Royals out.

We knew we were never out of the game with Cazzie ready to come in. My job was to look to get him off by getting the ball to him. Cazzie was a pure shooter, and, boy, he could fill it up when he got hot. He always assumed he was going to make the shot and he was really angry when he didn't. He had ultimate confidence in his shot. But even more important, Cazzie understood how to *get* a shot. He knew how to get open and get the shot off. Even if we hypothetically had wanted to freeze him out, he would still end up taking more shots than all of us put together. He wanted to score. When Cazzie was on a break, he always worked it out so that he'd end up with the shot. He'd pass you the ball just as a defensive man was coming, so that you'd have to give it back to him. Cazzie was very religious—occasionally quoting the Bible in the locker room, always going to church—so I guess he believed that God created him to shoot.

Cazzie was a show-off and a braggart, the type of guy who always had to be number one, and who wanted you to know about it. Still, I liked him. He was a lot of fun to have around, and in the locker room, he could work a give-and-go joke with Barnett and keep everybody laughing. Maybe he would've been a pain in the butt if I'd had to be around him all the time, but if you only see a guy a couple of hours a day—and if you don't hang around with him after the games are over—he's pretty easy to take.

While we were getting dressed, Danny Whelan called out from the other side of the room, "Hey, Muscles, you been eatin' all that wheat germ to build you up?"

Muscles Russell was the first health-food fanatic in the league. After the games, he would plug a little water heater into the outlet next to his stall and brew himself some herb tea. He worked out before it became popular, he took his vitamin pills, ate his wheat germ, and drank his herb tea—and he was always the first guy to catch a cold. "What's wrong with your tea, man?" Barnett would ask him. "Ain't getting enough wheat germ?" And then Cazzie, who could shout like a radio announcer most of the time, was quiet as a mouse.

With all his muscles, Cazzie never went anywhere near the boards. He could jump, but he wasn't going to get you any rebounds. He didn't like the contact. He was a strong guy, but he never physically intimidated anybody. His game was shooting the ball. I don't think he was scared of mixing it up under the boards; I think he just didn't care. He could shoot, and all he practiced was shooting the ball. After the team practice, Cazzie would go off by himself to the Y and shoot the ball some more.

The next day, the New York Mets won the World Series. What a good omen, I thought.

Cazzie was the heart of the bench, and the bench was strong a few nights later when we had a romp over Chicago. Riordan and Warren were in the backcourt, and Nate and the Rave and Muscles were up front. Even May and Hosket got in, and scored. All twelve guys on the team scored, yet somehow, we weren't comfortable. Red put all the starters on the bench by the third quarter, and still, we were scared. We knew you can't usually blow out a team for a whole game, and what happens if the guys on the bench blow the lead? Then you're out of the flow of the game, all the momentum is lost, and you have to go back in.

When the win finally looked solid, it was entertainment time, with Bowman as star performer. "Hey, man, that sucker don't know any of the plays," said Barnett, as Riordan tried to signal the Barry play to Nate. Nate didn't know Barry and didn't know the fist play or the cross or hardly any of them. Even Red was amused by it, and never fined him for not knowing. If we had been losing, he would've gotten on their butts. It wouldn't have been amusing then. If I'd thought about it seriously, it would have been frightening that Nate was our only real backup to Willis, but I wasn't thinking seriously then.

We waited for something to go wrong, and of course it did. Nate got the ball at the top of the key, went up for a jumpshot, showed perfect form, but the ball didn't leave his hands.

Nate had ability. He could jump, he was strong, he could do some things, but he was another one who never fulfilled his potential. He didn't like to practice too much and never tried to perfect his skills. In high school and even in college, natural ability frequently was good enough. You knew you didn't have to work at your game to be a star, to be better than most of the other guys. But when you go to the pros, everybody was that good, everybody had natural ability, and what made one player a star was just working at it more than the others. Players were like people in general; not many of them liked hard work. They didn't like to concentrate on things that were difficult for them to do. Most of them were happy enough just getting paid for doing something that came easily to them.

Like Stalls—maybe it was something they ate at Wichita State—Nate liked to party. He had more women on the line than anybody I've ever known. I roomed with him once and it was like working as an operator for the telephone company, taking his calls. "Uh, yes, Nate's not here right now.

41

Can I take a message?" No matter what hotel we walked into, no matter what city, there was always a loudspeaker announcement saying, "Telephone call for Mr. Bowman, telephone call for Mr. Bowman." Even though he was great with women, assured and always in control, Nate frequently seemed unsure of himself out on the court. When I roomed with him, he used to grind his teeth in his sleep. Maybe it was nerves. Maybe there was more going on inside Nate than we all suspected. In any case, a couple of years ago, Nate died, at much too young an age, from what I think was a heart attack.

The next night we faced the Lakers, who'd killed us the year before. This time, though, we held them under 100 points and managed to pull out a tight win. I went to the clubhouse and took my shower, and while I was still toweling off, I glanced at the stat sheet. The first thing I always looked for was how my man did. My man had been Jerry West. The stat sheet said West scored 42. Oh, man.

West had hit jumpers, lay-ups, offensive rebounds, just about anything he wanted. "You some defensive genius," Barnett started with me. Willis shouted over, "Where was Clyde tonight, Rich? Did Clyde come tonight? I don't believe I saw him out there." I felt bad, but I would have felt worse if we had lost. A win meant I could live with the guys getting on me.

"I thought you were a *dee*-fensive specialist, my man,"

Barnett went on. "How did this guy get forty-two on you? Never even seen that sucker before. You some specialist."

"Lucky you played him tough tonight, Clyde," Red added.

Forty-two points, that was not a good stat. West was a tough guy to shut down, and I was concerned. Still, what else could I do but smile? At least no one left dark glasses and a cane by my locker, which had been done once before.

We won four games in five nights and our first five in a row before playing San Francisco at the Garden. About halfway through the second quarter, Nate Thurmond argued a call too much and the ref threw him out. Thurmond was a horse. Of all the centers in the league, including Wilt and Kareem Abdul-Jabbar, who was then Lew Alcindor, Thurmond gave Willis the toughest time. He hounded him everywhere, went to the top of the key, out to the corners. Thurmond played defense and he rebounded, and he could score if you didn't guard him.

Out he went and in came someone named Dale Schleuter, about 6′ 10″ and thin and white. "This sucker," said Barnett, "betcha he got two moves. Backwards and forwards." Although no one said it, we figured we had the W. But our past history was that we played well against the good teams and had trouble with the lesser ones. Here it was happening again. Suddenly, we couldn't do anything. We seemed slow and out of sync. The Warriors started to get hot, even Schleuter, throwing up anything and getting it to fall. I could see that San Francisco was motivated: They were diving for balls, pushing us around under the boards. At halftime, Red was angry.

"How can you let a guy like this beat you?" he shouted. "This guy's no star. He shouldn't even be on the same *floor* with you, Willis. Clyde, you supposed to be an all-star. Your man is eating your ass up. Block the goddamn guy and get him off the boards. . . . " Red was screaming and he made you hate him. But no one said anything. We all just sat there and took it. We went out for the second half, didn't play any better, and lost to San Francisco. We were human.

CHAPTER

4

AFTER LOSING TO THE WARRIORS, WILLIS WAS extremely subdued. His eyes looked watery, like he was going to break out in tears. I think Willis understood that you're not going to win them all—he just hated to lose any of them. When I first knew him, the team used to do camps for kids in upstate New York, a day with the Knicks for the local children. We'd do, say, five different areas, put on a clinic at one camp early in the day, and then go on to another camp and sleep over. For a week or so, that was our job as professional basketball players. I went with Willis, Howie Komives, and Mike Riordan. At the end of the clinics, we'd play some one-on-one or two-on-two pickup games, just to illustrate some of the points we had made to the kids. If Willis lost, he'd go crazy. He'd pick up the ball and literally try to squeeze the air out of it, he was so mad. He'd slam it on the ground. He would stomp off to the side. I thought, This guy is nuts. This is just a meaningless pickup game.

Man, did he hate to lose. He is the most competitive guy I've ever known, and sometimes the angriest.

Willis was the first Knick player I met. I had just signed my rookie contract and was coming into New York for some publicity and to play some practice ball. Willis used to like to take rookies under his wing, so he picked me up at the airport, said "Hey, how you doin'?," and we got into his car. As we drove into the city, Willis was flooring it and the cops stopped us for speeding. Immediately, he got out of the car and started screaming and cursing at the cops.

"What the hell are you stopping me for? What kind of crap is this? What the hell do you think I was doing out here?"

Willis continued to curse and verbally abuse those cops, and I was so scared, I just slid down in my seat in the car. I was sure the cop was going to pull his gun out and shoot the captain of the New York Knicks. What a way to start my pro career: witness to a murder. But the cop didn't shoot Willis, after all; fact is, he didn't even give him a ticket.

Willis dropped me at my hotel and told me he was going to get me a date for that night, my first lady in New York City. Later, he picked me up and we rode down Broadway in his convertible, the first time I had ever been in one. The summer night was soft and peaceful, and I looked up and I could see stars over New York City. I'm going to buy me a convertible, I thought, and not much later, I did. We all went to Small's Paradise in Harlem that night. When Willis walked in, he got an ovation from the people there, and I even got a little applause, since I was the team's number-one draft pick. Oh, yeah, I thought, this is the life. And Willis was the Man. The big star of New York, and a real man all the way.

He was the captain, and he was in charge. He liked to take charge. He exuded authority, even the way he carried himself. That was the way he played, too. Willis was an over-achiever. He was not an exceptional jumper, and he wasn't that fast. But no one ever outhustled him—at practice, or during a game, or even at a kids' clinic. He had a great shot, particularly for a big man, and he was strong, and very quick, and smart, but what did it for him was desire. No one ever had a bigger heart than Willis Reed. As a player and a man, he was always on fire.

Everyone on the team liked Willis, and we all respected him. There was nothing he wouldn't do for his teammates. I wouldn't loan any of those guys my car. My things are personal to me. But Willis never thought twice about loaning his car, even the convertible, to anybody. "Hey, Will, you need the wheels tonight?" the Rave would ask. "No, man, you go take it and just drop it off here and I'll get it later." When Barnett or Cazzie needed money for gas, Willis would give it to them. If you needed to borrow some cash for something else, Willis's pockets were always open. Barnett was a steady customer, particularly when the card games were not going too good for Rich.

I thought Willis was almost a perfect person, at least until the fall of 1977. I was still playing, but Willis had retired and become the Knick coach. He did not have a great team to coach. Just before the season was going to begin, a Friday night, came a moment in my life that I'll never forget. I had just finished my weekly shopping at around six o'clock. I was living at Fifty-seventh Street and Second Avenue, and when I pulled into my driveway, I saw my agent then, Irwin Weiner, waiting for me. He had a look on his face like someone had died. I pulled up and rolled down my window.

"Hey, Irwin? What's up?"

"You've been traded."

I couldn't say anything but a quiet "Damn."

"It's Cleveland."

That just made it worse.

I never thought it would happen. Everybody gets traded. Oscar Robertson and Wilt got traded, and I knew that was the reality, but I never believed it would happen to me. And definitely not at that time. New York was my life, and I was the symbol of the Knicks. I had played well in preseason and led the team in scoring. I had seen Willis in the summer and he'd told me what good shape I was in. He said Ray Williams, who had been a number-one draft choice for the Knicks, was a good ballplayer, but I would still keep my job.

The season before, there had been a lot of rumors about Willis being named to coach. When he'd come to the games, he'd be quoted in the papers as saying that if he were running the team, he would trade Frazier. I just thought it was the press looking for a story, so I dismissed what I read. I had so much respect for Willis, I knew that if he had something to say to me, he would say it to my face.

When the trade came, Willis never said a word. He still hasn't. No one from Knick management ever told me directly about the trade.

I had had a good training camp, averaging around 21 points a game. I was coming off a mediocre season and had really worked out and prepared myself and felt I had something to prove. I felt I could still do all the things I had done before and wanted to show that to Willis. I thought I could play at least six more years.

Still, if Willis thought I was washed up, if he was seeing something that I wasn't and that the box scores weren't showing, he could have come to me and said, "Help me bring the young guys along. Work with Ray Williams." I would have been amenable to that. Instead, he just gave me away—for Jim Cleamons, a player not even remotely on my level.

I tried to understand it, but I couldn't. It didn't make any sense, and all I could think was that it was an ego thing. Maybe he just wanted me out of the way so he could be the team's focal point. I was the only other one there who was a link to how great the Knicks had been. I was still a star. Maybe Willis was jealous of me.

I had heard that he'd talked to other people about the trade, and told them that I couldn't do it anymore. Ten years later, when I was inducted into the Basketball Hall of Fame, all my old teammates were interviewed about me and my career. The press talked to Willis, and he was still saying what he had said a decade earlier. The trade was the best thing for me, he claimed. The Knicks were in trouble then, they had to go to a youth movement, and Cleveland had a better team than the Knicks did and I would fit in better there. I thought it was a lot of bullshit, and I didn't believe a word of it, then or now. Even after all those years, he still wasn't man enough to admit he had simply made a mistake. He wasn't big enough to say, "Hey, I was wrong and I should never have traded the guy," and left it at that. Or at least to say that he should have talked to me about it, explained it to me, since we had been through so much together.

Whenever we've bumped into each other since the trade, Willis has been friendly, and so have I. I still do consider him a friend—one mistake doesn't wipe out ten years—but I've never asked him about the trade and why he did it. I've never told him how I feel. I'm not comfortable displaying my emotions and, anyway, I don't think it's for me to bring it up. I understand it's a long time ago, and I don't work it over in my mind. Yet I haven't forgotten; it bothers me even today. It's a question of respect.

In the locker room after the Warrior loss, Barnett, who was usually jiving and joking, was as serious as Willis had been. He kept repeating, "Man, we can't let something like this happen to us again."

We didn't. Over the next five days, we won three in a row, and they were all blowouts. We beat the Bullets at the Garden, and the capacity crowd went crazy. They were screaming for us to hold Baltimore under 100 points, which we did, the fifth time in eight games we'd accomplished that. Defense was becoming our trademark, and the fans were recognizing that. Red was the first coach who stressed defense as a team tactic. He had made us realize that defense was our best offense. The Celtics had relied on defense, but they had Bill Russell. The Knicks were the first team where everybody played defense, and played it all over the court. When we'd call "red one," which meant, "Pick them up all over the court," you could see the other team get real fear in their eyes. Sometimes, even if we weren't going to press, I'd shout out "red one," which the other team knew, just to see if I could scare them. They'd suddenly stop and look around, to see where the press was coming from. I would just smile.

"Dee-fense, dee-fense," the crowd screamed. "Dee-fense, dee-fense," although we were up by almost thirty and the game was almost over.

I tipped the ball away from Earl Monroe, the hardest guy in the league for me to guard, and the fans screamed more than when we scored. Next time down, I stripped the ball from behind Gus Johnson; I was flying now. I couldn't stop. I was all keyed up, wanting to do it again and again. I wanted to flick the ball aside, strip it away, stuff my man. I couldn't get enough of defense. I usually tuned the crowd out, but for the first time, I really heard the crowd cheering and it psyched me up. I loved hearing them now because I got more pleasure from a steal than from a basket or a good pass. A steal is unique. No one is accustomed to seeing a guy just take the ball away from a professional player. With steals, I could disrupt a whole team's play. They had to think about where I was and change the way they operated. When I was stealing, I could control the game on both ends of the court.

I heard Gene Shue, the Bullets coach, shouting at Kevin Loughery, "Get Frazier out of there, move him away." Other coaches did it, too. They'd isolate me on the other side of the court with someone without the ball just so they could run a play. They were scared of my defense, and I loved it. I loved playing defense.

Everyone usually dreaded playing defense, but not me. It was easy for me. I had always had quick hands, my coaches as far back as high school always told me that. A conversation I once had with a friend about it became a New York legend. My friend told me his hands were "so fast I could catch a fly in midair."

So I told him, "That's okay, but I can catch two flies at a time."

He wanted to show me up, so then he said, "Well, man, I know a guy who can catch three at one time."

"That's pretty good," I told him, "but my trouble is that the flies have heard about me, and don't come around anymore."

In addition to the quick hands, I had good anticipation and a gambler's instinct on the court. I was always aware of seeing the ball and seeing my man, as Red would say. I had good peripheral vision. But mainly, it was pride. I hated to get beat. I took it personally when somebody scored on me. Sometimes, when I really wasn't into the game, when my mind was just floating and I was floundering, it took somebody scoring on me to get me moving. If somebody came down and scored on me two or three times in a row, it was like I'd been awakened from a dream. Suddenly, I was juiced, the way I needed to be. My blood was flowing now and I had to stop him, had to take the ball away from him.

To play defense, first, of course, you have to master the technique of the basic stance: It's a staggered stance, one foot behind the other, the same stance as if you're going to throw a punch at somebody. Your head's up, your butt's down. Your feet are shoulder-width apart and you're on the balls of your feet, not up on the toes or back on the heels. After you've mastered that, though, all defense is just pride and hard work. And I had worked hard on my defense.

For one full year at Southern Illinois, I played nothing but defense. Because of academic problems, I had lost my eligibility and couldn't play in what would have been my junior year. It was the first time in my life I couldn't play. Sports had been everything to me for a long time. That was the way I had wanted it, and I never had any regrets about it. By the time I was in the fourth grade, I was already playing basketball against sixth- and seventh-graders on the playground. The ball didn't bounce very straight on the dirt court, so you had to be a good dribbler to keep it going. After it rained, the soil would get matted and muddy and you had to know how to dribble over the bumps and rocks on the court.

When the older guys would shoot for nickels, they'd put me into the game for them. Talk about shooting under pressure. Being on the line in the NBA wasn't any harder than maybe letting down your friends when you're nine years old. I never got any of the money, but I rarely lost for them.

The older guys took me under their wing. They wouldn't let anybody rough me up, the way some of the players would try to do with the young kids. And when they were doing anything negative, they ran me on home. If they were shooting dice, or smoking, one of them would say, "Hey, man, you're going to be an athlete. You get on out of here."

Because of them and my mother, I never got into any trouble as a kid. My mother always said, "Don't ever do anything to destroy the family name." I never was where I shouldn't be, never got into any fights.

When I started playing on the school teams, the coaches would constantly preach to us that we had to be better than the white kids, twice as good as them just to be considered even. A lot of the kids in my schools were from the projects, and the only thing they took pride in was sports. The only way they could show they were good was to be the best. Our teams were perennial winners, and from grade school through high school, I was always captain of the team, in basketball, football, and baseball. In football, I was a quarterback who could throw left-handed as well as right-handed, and pass sixty yards on the fly, with great accuracy. In basketball, I was also all-city, but I didn't really know how good I was because I was just all-city against blacks. That wasn't enough, because when I read the *Atlanta Constitution,* I only read about white players and white teams.

I had never thought about going on to college. No one in my family ever had. But in my senior year in high school, everyone started asking me about it. Because of my mother, all the kids in the family had taken school very seriously. If we couldn't go one day because we were sick, we'd cry. All nine of us always had excellent school attendance records. I had been a B student until I got involved seriously in sports, and then my grades went down. When it came time to decide about going to college, I wasn't prepared, and I knew it. The white schools had all the best equipment and books. We got secondhand books, used and rejected, and our school didn't have any science labs or modern equipment. Teachers had said I should try to do better in my classes because I had an opportunity to win a scholarship, but I hadn't paid much attention. I didn't feel there was much incentive.

While there weren't any recruiters beating down my door, I did get some scholarship offers. A few white schools were interested in my playing football for them. I loved the game. My idol was Johnny Unitas, but I knew there wasn't a big market for black quarterbacks and that I didn't have the speed to be a wide receiver. It would have to be basketball. Kansas showed some interest, but only Tennessee State, an all-black school, really wanted me to play basketball for them. A friend tried to get me into Indiana, but neither my grades nor my test scores were good enough.

For blacks in the South who wanted to play sports back then, Tennessee State was the school, the home of the legendary Skull Barnett, who I'd know later as Dick Barnett. Right before I was set to follow another player from my high school to Tennessee State, a man who worked at my church,

Sam Johnson, told me he knew someone at Southern Illinois University. I had never heard of SIU, and they had never heard of me, but Sam could send me up for a visit.

My mother took me to the airport, and she was so proud, she was beaming. I was scared to death. It was my first airplane trip, and I don't think *she* had ever *seen* an airplane up close before.

The name of the town was Carbondale, Illinois, about a hundred miles south of St. Louis. It was a small town with about twenty-five thousand people, and it looked like all of them were white. The center of the town was the university, and I couldn't believe how big it was. Jack Hartman, the head coach, wasn't there when I visited, but the freshman coach had me scrimmage against some of the varsity players. He must have liked what he saw, because on the spot he offered me a one-year scholarship.

When I returned to Atlanta, my mother and sisters and brother all sat around the living room as I passed out the brochures I had gotten. They hung on every word I said. They were excited and so was I.

"I stayed in a whole town of white people," I told them. "I was in a Holiday Inn with white people all around and I was in a real fancy room, with my own bathroom, just for me."

Despite the excitement, I was still scared about going to Southern Illinois. I knew I didn't look like most of the people I saw there, and I didn't speak like them, either. I talked slower than they did, just like a black teenager from the Deep South would talk. I didn't think I could do the schoolwork, either. I knew from the SATs that there were a lot of things I didn't understand. I had sat there during the tests, trying to figure out the answers, and saying, Wow, man. I just didn't have any understanding of the stuff. I was scared of feeling lost.

My parents wanted Southern Illinois anyway, because, they said, it was a white school and I might get a better education there than at Tennessee State. I was apprehensive, but I did what they wanted. I was always a good child.

When my first college quarter began, I started to realize more completely what an inferior education I had received. I was a phys-ed major, and I got through that early time only because the team put me in a lot of easy courses. When basketball season started, I did all right with a little help from my friends on the team. Ed Zastrow, a white player on the freshman squad, became my best buddy, and we took as many classes together as we could, so he could help me with my studies.

I also got help from one of my teachers. I had attended every class of freshman speech, until it was *my* turn to give a speech. I was too shy to do it, and maybe too embarrassed at the slow, southern way I spoke. One day, I ran into the instructor, who could have flunked me, but instead asked to see me in his office.

"Why is it, Mr. Frazier," he wanted to know, "that you were in my class every day until it was time to give your speech?"

"I just can't talk in front of the class," I told him.

"You are the basketball player, right?"

"Yes, sir."

"Well, I have seen you play ball in front of a thousand people whom you *don't* know, so I can't understand why you can't talk in front of twenty people whom you *do* know."

That kind of made sense to me, so all I could think of to say was, "Well, I don't know what to speak on."

"Why not give a speech on basketball?"

Okay. The first speech I ever gave in college—or for that matter, anywhere—was on basketball and the fundamentals of playing it. From then on, I gave a speech every week when I was called on.

Still, I was more comfortable on the basketball court than in the classroom. Jack Hartman was a strict disciplinarian, and I liked that. All my other coaches had been tough, so I was used to it. Hartman believed in the fundamentals and that everybody had to follow the same rules. He wouldn't take any junk from anybody, even when he was wrong. I didn't particularly like him. But I respected him.

After a few weeks of team practice, Hartman called me into his office. He only had three full four-year scholarships to give out that year, but he told me I could have the last one of the three. It seemed to hurt him to say it.

The scholarship gave me fifteen dollars. A month. But in those days, that was a lot. It only took a couple of dimes to do your wash, and another dime to dry the clothes. It was fifty cents for a big pizza, and all the Coke I could drink was another quarter. The movies also cost a quarter, but only if I didn't have a free pass. To add to the scholarship, I worked, all the time. When all the other students would go home for the holidays, for Christmas or Thanksgiving, for long and even short weekends, I stayed and worked in the dorms. If I had wanted to return to Atlanta, I would have had to ride a train for fifteen hours. That was assuming my parents had the money to send for me. I didn't want to be a burden to my family. I really hated to write home for money. Rather than bug them, I just wouldn't go home—except during the summer—and would earn as much money as I could myself. I'd clean rooms or work in the laundry or in the cafeteria, or do any job the people at school had for me. Added to the money I earned, from time to time my uncle would send me ten bucks and maybe another relative or friend would send me five more. By the end of the month, I had around fifty dollars, and it was like paradise. I felt rich. I felt I had so much money left over at the end of the month,

I could go shopping and buy myself some new clothes. I did. They were good buys, too.

My first year on Hartman's varsity, I led the team in scoring, averaging almost 25 points a game. By the end of the year, though, I started to get cocky. I felt Hartman and some of the players had it in for me. I thought I wasn't getting the ball enough, and then, suddenly, Hartman benched me, without saying a word to me about why. When we played Evansville, our arch rival, Hartman, who had me sitting, told me to go in when the game got tight. I was so angry and upset about not playing, I had literally made myself sick. I had been okay before the game, but now I felt dizzy and lethargic. I just sat there. Hartman repeated it: Get on in.

"Hey, man," I said, "I'm sick. I can't go in." He turned livid, but didn't say another word then. At halftime, he told me that if I was sick, I shouldn't go out on the floor for the second half.

I rarely got off the bench again that season. I was so angry about what had happened, I started to say to hell with everything. I didn't care. I had been doing okay in my classes, but now I stopped going. I was unhappy with what was happening on the court, so what was the point in going to class? I no longer wanted to be at Southern Illinois, and I planned on leaving college at the end of the year. When I left Carbondale at the close of classes, I didn't tell anyone, but I knew it was all over for me there.

Back home, I started hanging out in the old neighborhood, around Edgewood and Auburn, just down the street from Martin Luther King's church. I saw some of the guys I'd played with in high school. They had always seemed to have lots of money back then, while I was busy trucking bales of cotton. They had big flashy cars, and I'd felt embarrassed in front of them. Now, they were just hanging out on the corners. Willie Fleetwood, who had been the star basketball player at Howard High after me, was getting fatter and fatter. He looked like he weighed 250. I asked someone where my friend Al was, and they told me he was in jail. Other guys were in jail, too, and some were on dope. I knew I didn't want that. I knew, then, that I wanted to go back to school, someplace.

My mother wanted me to go back to SIU. Hartman never called or had any contact with me that summer. But the athletic director asked me to come back and give it another shot. I wasn't thrilled about giving SIU another try, but I did. And it was the making of me as a person. I went back to the school, but I had to sit out one year of basketball because of my academic record. During that year I sat out, no one from the basketball program helped me out. No one enrolled me. I had to take tough subjects, a full load of heavy courses, and no garbage classes to balance them. No P.E. courses at all. If I flunked out, okay, but I was going to give it a good shot. This was going to make me or break me. I made a 3.8 grade-point average that quarter. Hey, I realized, I'm not so dumb.

I wasn't able to play on the team that season, but Hartman let me practice with it. He wouldn't let me touch the ball on offense, though. I had to play defense every day, just guarding the team's starters. After about two weeks, I finally understood that I wasn't going to distinguish myself that season by shooting and scoring. Okay, I decided, if he's going to do that, then I'm going to be the best damn defensive player he ever saw. I began to realize that playing defense was more than just quickness and reflexes and instinct. You had to be smart to play defense. You had to watch your man, see what he does. Find out his habits and tendencies. When you play against the same guys day after day, you have to do that. Finally, when you can sense what's going to happen, you gain that split-second advantage. Then it's the quickness and the reflexes that take over.

Hartman had the first team run their plays against me and four other substitutes. I was so effective stealing the ball they couldn't run them. We didn't just try to stop the starters from scoring. We didn't want them to be able to bring the ball upcourt against us. We tried to humiliate them, and we did. When they couldn't do anything at all against us, that would really annoy Hartman. "Stop fouling so much!"

he'd scream. I knew I wasn't fouling. Finally, he'd get so annoyed at me, he'd say, "Frazier, sit down." I really got to him, and for a year, that was my gratification, my only gratification.

Defense had become my game. Even when I started with the Knicks, I had confidence that I could stop anybody. On offense, I was frequently scared and unsure, but I knew I had the ability to defend against anyone. That first Knick team was in so much turmoil, I knew I had to play defense if I wanted to play at all. It was just like being back at SIU. Once I passed the ball, I never saw it again. Some guys on that team were like black holes; no balls ever came back from them. The only way to make my mark was by showing I could do it defensively.

After we blew out Atlanta, going 8–1 on the young season, I sat down in front of my two-and-a-half-foot-wide cubicle and started to peel off my clothes. The locker room was quiet, nobody saying very much, except to the reporters hanging around. Red came in and said quietly, "Good game, guys," and moved on. As always, the ball boys had a bucket of ice waiting for me so I could soak the arthritic toe on my right foot. I put on my jacket so I wouldn't catch a cold. Over at the entrance to the room there was suddenly a lot of noise. In walked Adam Clayton Powell, the king of Harlem. He was trailing people behind him, his driver and a woman who might've been his secretary. With his deep preacher's voice, I could hear him easily.

"I am," he was announcing to some of the reporters, "the official chaplain of the New York Knickerbockers."

I knew Adam a little, because he was a fan and hung out downstairs at the Garden club, and had invited me to dinner a few times. With me, he wasn't serious, always a fun-loving kind of guy, not the dangerous militant most white people thought he was. But he had that reputation, and the next day, a lot of people were upset and demanding to know why he had been allowed into the Knicks' locker room.

Adam was a big fan, and there were a lot of them now. The Knicks had been making basketball fashionable. Elliott Gould and Woody Allen had been coming to all the home games, and I always saw Soupy Sales sitting right behind the Knicks bench. DeBusschere was hanging out with Robert Redford. The Knicks were the rage.

In a newspaper interview, Joe Lapchick, the former Knick coach and a member of the Basketball Hall of Fame, was quoted as saying we were the greatest basketball team he had ever seen. Hey, man, slow it down. We were talking about a month or so worth of the season. What had we won already?

Things were swirling around us, but the locker room

seemed no different than it used to be. Just as quiet as before. Somebody asked, "Hey, you see this article in the paper?" And somebody answered, "Yeah, and it ain't worth a thing. What happens, man, if we lose five in a row? The fans are fickle, man. We lose one game and then we are the worst they ever saw."

With San Diego coming into the Garden to play us, I read the sports section of the papers that afternoon looking to see if there was anything about me in there. There was. The Rockets coach said that I was "an awkward type player, but he seems to get the job done." That night, I came down-court on one of our first possessions and hit from way out. Then I hit another jumper from the top of the key as I was falling down. And another. The basket was ten feet wide. I started to figure I could throw up anything, bounce it off my nose, and it would go in. After the first five or six baskets, I lost track, in the flow of the game, of how many I was scoring. In the fourth quarter, Willis was shouting at me, "Take some shots, man. Keep shooting it, keep shooting it."

The game felt so easy, so effortless. I felt like I was in a trance, floating through the evening. This is so much fun, I said to myself. Why can't it be like this every night?

We won easily, and when it was over, I had no sense of how many points I'd scored. I figured it was around 25 or maybe 30. I took a look at the stat sheet and there it was: 14

of 22 from the floor, 15 of 19 from the line. Forty-three points, my career high.

"Have you ever scored that many in a game before?" the reporters asked me.

"I've never scored that many points even warming up," I told them. "I always look for the open man," I went on, "and tonight I was the open man." I liked being clever and giving the reporters good quotes and being quoted by them, and then reading the words I had said. All people like reading about themselves, and like most ballplayers, I felt that if I wasn't in the paper, why read it? I wanted to find out what people were saying about me and what they thought of me. Sometimes, of course, the words I read weren't exactly the words I had said, but I really didn't care. Some reporters were okay; with others, you'd tell them one thing, but when it was in print, it looked different. For that reason, reading the sports section of some New York papers would be comic relief during the season. Many of the New York reporters thought they could coach the team and would try to prove it every day with a story. They gave their opinions of what the Knicks should do, how we should play, and what I was doing right, and most of all, what I was doing wrong. Since I liked reading about myself, most of the time when I was criticized I could accept it. I figured that when I was going good, they made me a hero, so now, if I was bad, I couldn't complain. That was part of the game.

We all knew the press had favorites. I'd always hang around until all the reporters had gotten a shot at me, so they treated me pretty well. But Willis was their pet. The Knicks' PR people were tight with him, and one of them was even partners with Reed in a kids' camp. He was the guy they promoted. Whenever there was something to be done, they made sure Willis did it. If there was a Knick up for a commercial, they made sure Willis got it. It wasn't that he didn't deserve it; Willis was the team's star: the captain and the leader and a great player. But in creating the image of Willis Reed, he also had help. The PR people, who were sort of an extension of the press, worked for that image, and the reporters were happy to accept it. He became the team's spokesman, and the reporters rarely if ever wrote anything negative about him.

Barnett, who never much liked talking to the press, always got ripped by the reporters. They thought he was a moody guy and a selfish player—which he may have been once, but sure wasn't anymore. They saw him on the court where he was deadly serious, hardly ever smiling. They perceived him as just a gunner who wasn't concerned with anything but scoring his points and making money, and Rich never tried to change that perception. He never cared about his image. Maybe early in his career the press wrote things about him that turned him off. He had come into the league when there were very few blacks playing, and I think he felt he never got his due from the white media. Now, when he was asked something by a reporter, he would give abrupt answers. Yeah, no, I don't know. A reporter would throw a six-sentence, two-minute question, and Rich would answer it with, "Yeah, that's right." And all the time, he'd barely look up at the reporter and never smile.

I think maybe that's the reason that of all the guys who played a major part on that team, Barnett's the only one who hasn't had his uniform number retired by the Knicks. My jersey is hanging in the Garden, as well as Willis's, DeBusschere's, and Bradley's. The only starter on the 1970 team whose uniform isn't there is Barnett's. It should have been retired, he deserved the honor, but a lot of those things are just popularity contests. And Barnett was never very popular with the people who counted, like the team management and the press.

Of course, two seconds after the reporters left the locker room, Barnett would start rapping, and he was hilarious, the funniest man I ever met in basketball.

I first knew of him as Skull Barnett. Any black man over forty years old remembers Skull Barnett. At Tennessee State, he had a bald head and was a legend throughout the South, one of the all-time great scorers and all-around ballplayers. I never got to see him play, but my Uncle Eddie had, and he told me about the time Skull walked into the Tennessee State campus cafeteria and all the students stood up and gave him a standing ovation.

When the reporters weren't there, Barnett would be at center stage, telling stories about the old days at Tennessee State, when "we were on the road again." He'd talk it out real slow, dragging every word. His face was deadpan and his eyes were almost closed, but he'd have a funny kind of smile on his lips.

"See, the game here is now on the line in the last ten seconds. We are down by one, and I'm dribbling into the front court. I got about thirty-five already, it bein' an off night. I'm shakin' men all over the floor. I get to the top of the key and I make a move to my left. My man goes for the fake so much, he falls dead on his ass. I make another move to my right, and another chump hits the dust. I go up with a fall-back baby and just as I pull the trigger, the fuckin' lights go out. Shoulda made it anyway, but it hits the back rim, at least that's what it sounds like, and just as it's comin' down, the lights come back and the buzzer goes off. We lose.

"'Course, that weren't as bad as when we played where they didn't have no nets on the baskets. We're scorin' all over the place and the other guys are sayin' the ball's not goin' in. You can't see it, so they's no way to prove anythin'. And, man, it's their court, and their refs, and so the ball don't go in. Ain't nuthin' you can do. So I naturally did the only thing I could, I started bankin' the muthas in."

On the court, Barnett didn't fool around, even though he did look funny shooting that weird jumper of his. He called it fall-back baby because as he was shooting it, before the ball even reached the basket, he'd say, "Fall back, baby." It meant, Let's get back on defense. This is two points, my man. I had thought the shot was crazy, but then I studied it. Barnett's elbows were straight, and he was facing the basket. The only part that was different was his legs, which were folded underneath him and which he kicked when he released the ball.

Rich could score from anywhere with that shot. He came into the league with a scorer's reputation, and the teams he played on wanted him to shoot and score. At the beginning of his pro career, the word on him was that he wouldn't pass the ball to his mother. When Dick McGuire was the Knick coach, Barnett was his designated gunner. When Red came in, he said, "Everybody plays defense," and that meant Barnett, too. Red put him in a precarious position, an older guy who had to run and chase the young players all over the court. Barnett knew that if he didn't hustle on defense, he was gone. If he didn't become a team player, good-bye. In a sense, though, he had good timing going for him. With his career near the end, he understood that he would have to make adjustments, and was willing to make them. Rich learned to play defense, and he played it tough, very physically. He was the team's old man, but he ran the court as well as anybody on the club. Because he stayed in shape and never smoked or drank, he probably prolonged his career by three or four years.

He became a team player, but he never lost his ability to score. I guarded him in practice, and he still had all the moves. There was one in particular where he faked the shot, got the defender off his feet, and then pushed out his shoulder and jumped into him as he went up again, getting the basket and the foul. It gave me so much trouble in practice, I said, Hey, I should use this myself, too. And I did.

I also learned about fashion from Barnett. He was one of the first sharp dressers in the league, everything coordinated and custom-made. He took me out to Brooklyn to his personal shirt-maker, and I started going there regularly, too. I liked the fabrics. Barnett definitely had flair.

We had won four in a row when the Bucks came to the Garden. The year before, they had been horrendous. There was an advantage to being so bad, though. They had gotten the rights to Lew Alcindor in the draft. I hadn't played against him in college, but I had seen enough of him. He was probably the most dominant college player who ever lived. What impressed me most was how methodical he was.

He seemed oblivious to everyone on the court, as if he were alone, playing by himself. It seemed there wasn't anything he couldn't do on a basketball floor.

When we got out on the court, the first thing that struck me about Alcindor was how tall he was. Willis was listed as 6′ 9″ or 6′ 10″, but it was obvious that Lew was more than half a foot taller than Willis. When you are 7′ 2″ or 7′ 3″ or whatever, I thought, it doesn't matter what your vertical leap is.

I always got the feeling that Lew was sensitive about his height. A couple of years later, at an all-star game in Philadelphia, I gave him a ride in my car. It was a big Cadillac Eldorado, and I kept trying to adjust the front seat so he could get into the back and be comfortable. He kept saying, "No, I'm all right, man, don't worry, don't worry." But his knees were up in his chest as he tried to get into the car, and he sat awkwardly throughout the ride and never said a word.

It's tough being that tall. I know I'll never meet him at a bar again. We once talked for a long time in a little bar on New York's Upper West Side. To have a conversation with a seven-footer, you have to look way up and get close to talk. By the time he left, I had a terrible crook in my neck.

As the game began, Willis, who probably wasn't even the height he was listed as, looked so small next to Lew, it was a little scary. What was even scarier was how Lew played. He was shooting the sky hook, spinning to the basket, slamming

73

it down. He did it all so easily, I thought, What would it be like to be seven feet tall and dominate the game like he's doing? How would it feel, just once, to be able to jump into the basket? When I scored 43 points, I worked like a dog to get them. But Lew dominated nonchalantly.

In a very few minutes, Willis was in foul trouble from trying to guard him. In came Nate Bowman. It didn't matter that Nate didn't know the plays or that he was probably not in great shape. Nate was awkward, like a duck, and Lew was having trouble with him. Nate was never reacting exactly like Lew thought he should, and that was an advantage for Nate. Lew had never played Nate, and so didn't know what to expect from him. Nate, who could always jump, seemed to be jumping higher than normal. Yet he was playing within himself, intelligently, passing off when he should and going to the hoop when he could. He even blocked one of Alcindor's shots and won a jump ball from him. Near the end of the game, it was Alcindor who looked a little tired and out of it. He ended up with over 30 points and almost 30 rebounds, but Nate got enough points and boards back for us, and we won our fifth game in a row.

Afterward, it was Nate who was the press's favorite. He gave all the interviews, explaining to the reporters that this was only *one* of his better games. (I wondered when the other one was.) Willis, who had been completely overshadowed on the court, was now completely overshadowed in the locker room. He sat quietly. In two nights, we'd be playing the Bucks again, in Milwaukee.

"Our man is getting ready," Barnett said. The next game would be payback. The next game was on the road.

CHAPTER 5

I HATED TO PLAY IN MILWAUKEE. I THOUGHT IT WAS drab city, the worst arena in the league, the quietest, most polite, whitest crowd, and the worst baskets in the NBA. The baskets were so tight that when you shot and hit the rim, the ball went *boing*. I always knew when we played there that I was going to get a lot of rebounds because the balls would bounce so far out, where I and the other little guards could get to them.

No matter where we played, the baskets were always different, and you had to adjust to them. Some rims were loose and gave a good bounce if you could get the ball to hang up there. Each arena had baskets designed for the home team, like in baseball, where they let the grass grow long if the home team could bunt well. It was a way of getting a little edge. In Baltimore, since the Bullets were a running team, they had long, loose nets, so the ball would fall straight through quickly and the Bullets could be off and sprinting. At Madison Square Garden, the nets were new and short, so they would be a little tighter than usual. As a team that mostly shot from the outside, we wanted the ball to get stuck in the net so the other team couldn't take it out of bounds and fast-break quickly upcourt. The slow nets let us get back on defense.

Milwaukee also wasn't exactly a hip place to play. In the cities with large black populations, like Detroit and Baltimore, there was always a festive mood to the crowd. The people were usually all dressed up and wanted to show it off, sashaying up and down the aisles before the game and during halftime. The women had their best jewelry to flash around, and everybody trailed thick fur coats behind them. The black crowds were more vocal, with lots of oohs and aahs when there was a spectacular dunk or a sharp behind-the-back pass. In Baltimore and Detroit and Philadelphia, there were rock and soul blaring from the loudspeakers. In Milwaukee, we had a marching Dixieland band.

Tonight Willis didn't seem to mind the rims, or the crowd, or the music. He seemed psyched from the opening tap. On defense, he bodied Alcindor and kept pushing him farther and farther away from Lew's favorite spot. When Lew tried to go left, Willis forced him right. On offense, Willis shot that little left-handed jumper of his, and Lew didn't challenge him. He didn't want to come out from the basket, and Willis stood there, at twelve feet, at fifteen feet, and kept popping. Alcindor finally went out a little, and Willis, the best shooting big man I've ever seen, retreated a couple of steps and hit some more.

More than the shooting, and his quickness and strength, it was Willis's pride that won this night. He had been embarrassed by Alcindor in New York, and he couldn't wait until he had another shot at him. Lots of players in the league had pride, but few of them wanted revenge like Willis did. Willis wanted to be the best center in the NBA, and wanted everybody to know he was the best center. To be the best, he knew he had to prove it against the best, against Alcindor, and Wilt, and Thurmond.

Willis got 35 points and held Lew to 17 as we beat the Bucks again. The Knicks were now off to the best start in the franchise's history, said the newspapers the next day. We were 11 and 1, with six in a row, as we headed off to the West Coast for nine days and four more on the road.

I traveled light for the trip, carrying just one very large bag. Earlier in my pro career, I took a lot of suitcases on trips and loaded them all with as many clothes as I could stuff in them. I wanted to look good wherever I went. I carried the bags myself, and my arms used to kill me from lugging them all around. I learned that good packing was the essence of good traveling. A friend named Billy Jackson taught me how to fold all my things very neatly and make them as compact as possible, so I could cut down on the number of bags.

I also stopped being stingy. When we arrived at the hotels on the road, I got my room key in the lobby and immediately would signal for a bellhop and have him lug my heavy bag all the way to the room. I wasn't going to kill myself anymore to save a buck or two.

Ballplayers are notoriously cheap, and that's the way I had been, too. We were cheap because we were spoiled. Since high school and college, we were accustomed to being given everything and never having to pay for it. The drinks were always on somebody, and free tickets were always handed to us. We got out of the habit of paying. Ballplayers are always the last guys to put out for a meal or to buy a suit. They always want it free because they usually can get it free. The idea is to absolutely avoid spending any money if you don't have to. Even though ballplayers make a lot more today, I bet you they're still the same way.

In New York, the Knicks paid the bill for those of us— me, Bowman, Stallworth, and some others—who lived at the New Yorker. The team even reimbursed us for taxis when we had to go to the airport or to practice somewhere in Queens. Of course, we never failed to take advantage of management's generosity. All four or five of us made sure to take separate taxis out to the airport or to the practice sites. I guess management eventually got wise to us, because they decided to stop reimbursing us for the cabs. From that moment on, we all piled into the same taxi for the trips. It was never too comfortable, but hey, it was now our own money, and at least it was a lot cheaper.

Most everybody on the team hated going on the road. Not me. All the other guys thought about was that you don't sleep in your own bed, you don't drive your own car. The numbers of the TV channels are different and you can't get the *Daily News* or *New York Post*. You're not comfortable, the way you are at home. Yeah, sure, life on the road was lonely, but that's exactly why I liked it. I liked being alone. With eight sisters and a brother, I never had a chance as a kid to be a loner. There was never any privacy back home in Atlanta. Now, finally, I could have a hotel room practically all to myself.

My roommate on the road trip was Donnie May, and I hardly ever saw him. He was always out doing something, maybe just going for a walk or sightseeing, and so the room was mine. Donnie and I never had much to do with each other, although he was an okay guy. I think it was cultural. He was white, from Dayton, Ohio, the last guy on the bench and the most meticulous person I ever met. Normally, when you come into a hotel room, the guys will throw their bags right in the closet, never use the dresser or the shelves. Just spread everything out, and when you need something, go try to find it. Not Donnie May. In our hotel room, everything was neat. Donnie hung up all his clothes in order, color-coordinated. In the bathroom, he had his deodorant, his toothbrush, his hairbrush, and his comb perfectly in line. When he left the room, he made sure to always have his bed completely made and his hair combed just right. It was disgusting. He kept me neat for a while, but I couldn't take that kind of pressure for long. Eventually, I reverted to my normal nature. It was good that Donnie left me alone most of the time.

The Knicks were the only team in the league that still had roommates. DeBusschere and Bradley were together, Cazzie and Barnett, the Rave and Nate, Willis and Johnny Warren, because Reed always liked to hang with the rookies and show them around. That left me the odd man out, because I would room with anybody, it didn't matter. My only request was no smokers. We were the last team to room singly, because the players didn't mind. We didn't necessarily have to have separate rooms, and Donnie wasn't the only white roommate I ever had on the team. Phil Jackson and I were also together for a while. We were called "the Odd Couple," the talkative, awkward-looking white guy from North Dakota, and the shy, smooth black from Georgia. We weren't that different, though. Phil was a free spirit who liked to have a good time. He was cool. We came to the team the same year, two rookies who didn't know anything or anybody, and as soon as we hit a new town, we'd drop our bags and go sightseeing together. Neither of us had ever seen San Francisco, and there was no way we were going to miss the

Golden Gate Bridge and Alcatraz. We had good times together. Phil and I became pretty tight.

I liked rooming with white guys. This is nothing against blacks, but black guys like it hot. A black comes into the hotel room, the first thing he does, he turns up the heat. Then he closes the windows. It's winter and the room feels like 100 degrees. White guys are just the opposite. With them, the room is always freezing. No matter how cold it is, the whites will always crack a window. The heat just saps you, and there's not much you can do about it. It's a lot easier to adjust to the cold.

When we hit the hotel in Phoenix, the white guys went to hang out down by the pool, to work on their tans. Bowman, the Rave, and a few of the other blacks eventually headed for a nearby discotheque they could walk to. Except for the game, I stayed in the room, listening to some Motown, watching TV, resting and relaxing. There's only so much energy I have in my body, and I wanted to hold on to it until I needed to use it. I was too lazy even to get up and go downstairs to the hotel restaurant for my meal. It wasn't just laziness. I also didn't want to bump into the other guys down at the restaurant. They'd be running the poor waitress all over the place, and then leave her a quarter for a tip. If they were already eating and I got there last, it was a sure thing they'd try to stick me with the tab. You want to eat with pro ballplayers, always make sure you get there first—and get up from the table first. As usual, I ordered up from room service, and as usual, it was terrible. I never understood why room service food was always worse than what you got in the restaurants, even if it was from the same kitchen. For a couple of hours afterward, the room service food lay in my stomach like a fat beached whale.

In general, ballplayers don't eat very well. There's no time to eat, so you grab what you can. Your body is so highly trained and in such good shape you figure no matter what you eat, it's not going to hurt you. You're always stuffing in a hamburger or a hot dog before catching a plane or going out to the arena. Bradley couldn't stop eating sweets, whenever he got the chance. With the exception of Cazzie, nobody cared anything about diet or knew very much about good nutrition. I wasn't any different. I ate as much red meat as I could, and I never met a vanilla ice cream I didn't like. My idea of health food was a double scoop, hold the sprinkles.

When the phone rang for a few minutes, I just let it ring, maybe a couple of dozen times. I didn't have to talk to anybody on the road. Nobody could bug me if I didn't want to be bugged. The road was an escape. My only responsibility was to be ready for the game.

We got to San Diego after another win, with a couple of days to kill before we played the Rockets. We would practice the next day, so Red gave us the travel day off. I didn't have to conserve my energy, so I decided to take advantage of the free time. With a few of the guys on the team, we rented a car and went down to Tijuana, where I'd never been and have no desire to go back to. We were on the lookout for an act we had heard about, featuring a donkey and a woman. At least that's what somebody had said we could find in Tijuana.

We walked down the filthy main street with hustlers trailing behind us, trying to sell us everything they could think of. We kept asking if anybody knew where we could see the act with the donkey and the woman, but I guess their English wasn't great and our Spanish wasn't too good, either. We went into a bar to get away from the dirt and the heat and the hustlers, but I wouldn't drink anything, not even a beer. Not in Tijuana. On the counter of the bar was a nude lady dancing right in front of us. She swayed back and forth, spreading different parts of her anatomy in new and various ways, until it was clear we'd had enough of that.

We went back out on the street, still searching for our donkey. Finally, a guy said, Yeah, I know where you can see it. So we piled into his car and he drove us all the way out of town to a pretty ratty-looking house. We walked in and were immediately surrounded by women. They were not young. One latched onto me; and she was probably the oldest of them all. It eventually became obvious to us all that we were in a not very classy whorehouse. We got out of there fast. We got out of Tijuana, too, without ever finding the donkey or the woman. Life on the road can be tough.

The Lakers looked different out on the court. Jerry West was warming up and Elgin Baylor, too, but there was no Wilt. Two days before, while we were beating San Diego, Chamberlain had torn up his knee. The reports were that he was going to be out for the season, or at least for a couple of months. There was even some talk that he would never come back, a ruptured tendon being a pretty severe injury. I figured, though, that he'd be back. Wilt was just about indestructible, by far the strongest man in the league. If anyone could come back, he could.

Instead of Wilt out on the floor, the Lakers had a rookie named Rick Roberson playing center. Willis took him to school, and the rookie got more and more frustrated. In the second half, Roberson went up for a rebound under the Laker basket and threw an elbow out in frustration. In connected with DeBusschere's nose. Dave fell hard to the floor, and blood was coming from his nose. He got up slowly and headed to the bench, where Danny tried to stop the bleeding by putting his fingers all around and over Dave's nose. Dave was one of the toughest ballplayers I've ever seen, but he also didn't like pain very much. He had a very low threshold for it, just the opposite of Willis. Willis once got hit in the face during a game, came out and said very casually to Danny, "Hey, I think my nose is broke." He said it like you or I would say, "Hey, I think I tore my nail a bit." Then Willis sat down, Danny pushed his nose back in place, and Willis returned to the game.

Dave and Willis were the kind of guys who would get their noses broken. That's the risk they took when they went in there under the basket with all those big guys. Me, I never got anything broken, because I made sure to always keep my nose out of it. Of course, if it *had* happened to me, I would have gotten very upset. How do I look? I would have asked people. Is it going to affect my profile? With a broken nose, I would at least have gone to the locker room to look in the mirror and see what had happened to my face. But Willis just went right back in the game.

I guess Dave is a little more like me. Danny maneuvered his nose around and Dave was screaming, "Take it easy, take it easy."

"It's broke," Danny told him. "You want me to straighten it out for you?"

"Are you kidding me?" Dave asked. "Take me to the goddamn hospital."

Dave went off to the local hospital, and Stallworth came in off the bench, nailed a few shots, and pulled down some key rebounds, and we won again.

Right before Christmas in 1968, we were in Detroit, with a day off before we were going to play the Pistons. I was in my hotel room, sitting in bed and watching TV, when the news came on and I heard the announcement that the New York Knicks had traded Walt Bellamy and Howie Komives for Detroit's Dave DeBusschere. I turned off the TV. I was dumbfounded, incredibly surprised the Knicks had made the trade. This was not a good move, I said to myself, not at all. We had been doing okay, why shake things up so much?

I didn't even think about DeBusschere himself at first. What immediately hit me was that we were giving up our starting center and a starting guard, both good players, and right away, the trade made Detroit a quality team. But what did it do for us? Reed would now have to move over to center, and some of us wondered if he could be a dominant force there. Everybody knew that DeBusschere wasn't having a great season. He wasn't too old, he was only twenty-eight, but maybe he had burned himself out already. Up until five years earlier, he had played both pro basketball for the Pistons and pro baseball for the Chicago White Sox organization, and he had always played extremely hard, no matter which sport. And then for three years he had been the Pistons' player-coach, and that can age any man fast. I had seen guys who had carried a lot smaller burden burn themselves out by the age of twenty-five and have nothing left afterward. The word around the league was that DeBusschere wasn't on the way up, he was on the way out. I had heard that he had a bad back, and anyway, he was a Detroit guy—he had played college ball at the University of

Detroit—and had been one all his life. So if he was playing so well and in such good shape, tell me, why did they want to trade him?

The day after the trade was announced, the Knicks and Pistons played each other at Cobo Hall. Dave hadn't practiced with us or even met some of the guys on the team. I don't remember the numbers anymore, but Dave was easily the best player on the floor that night, over 20 points and a load of rebounds. We played maybe our best game of the season, beating the Pistons by close to 50 points. Hey, maybe it wasn't such a bad trade after all.

It was obvious that DeBusschere didn't play like a guy on the way down. Every minute he was on the floor, he hustled, sweating and deep-breathing all the way up and down the court. He took the shots when they were there, but he never forced anything. It was like he had been playing with us for years.

After the game, I heard him talking to the press. Every time he mentioned the Pistons, he called them "we." "Hey, man," I told him, "the Knicks are *we* now."

From literally that first game and the first practice, the Butcher gave us things we hadn't had. He gave us a forward who could shoot the ball and could pass the ball, and an unselfish player who complemented Reed perfectly.

Bells—Walt Bellamy—and Willis had an ego problem together. They were always fighting for the same rebounds and getting in each other's way. Bells, who was bigger, was a natural center who could only play with his back to the basket, and had pushed Willis out to forward. Willis had defensive problems there and didn't like having to go up against faster, quicker forwards. Bells didn't like sharing the middle. Willis, who played hard from the moment he walked out of the locker room, thought that Bells didn't always put out, which was basically true, of course. Like Willis, I thought he was a bad influence on the younger players, because they would see that he didn't always play hard and wonder why they should. Bells only did what he had to do to hang around. Some nights I thought he must have had a date, so he would get himself thrown out of the game in the first couple of minutes. Sometimes he would seem to foul intentionally, just so he could sit and rest on the bench. Yet against Russell or Chamberlain, he'd go all out, play terrific, and give them a hard time. It was obvious on those nights that he was one of the best centers in the league. But the next game, somebody like Tom Boerwinkle would get 30 on him, and it was like Bells wasn't there. Bells and Willis were not the same kind of player. They did not function well together and did not want to function together.

The Butcher, on the other hand, worked well with Reed, because he was a lot like Willis as a player. He didn't mind doing the dirty work. He busted his butt all the time. He wasn't a great jumper, but he always worked hard. He banged bodies, and he never backed down to anybody. Players like Gus Johnson on the Bullets and the Sixers' Luke Jackson, tough and aggressive and taller and strong, physically intimidated other forwards. Guys would give them an extra step or two because they didn't want to have to bang with them. Dave wasn't one of those guys. Nobody intimidated Dave.

If he wanted a rebound, Dave would just push the other guy out of the way, but never get caught doing it. Better than anyone else I've ever seen, he understood the fundamentals of boxing out. Just as the shot was taken, Dave would immediately find his man and get his body into him. He'd hook him there, and keep him there. Then he'd find the ball. It doesn't matter if you aren't a great jumper if your man doesn't have a chance to get the ball. Dave perfected that, and it's something very few players in today's NBA know how to do. They know they can all run and jump out of the gym, and so they feel they don't have to box out the way DeBusschere used to. They just stand there under the hoop and let small forwards like Charles Barkley go over them and lead the league in rebounding. Small forwards didn't lead the league in rebounding back then. Many of the top rebounders in the league today aren't even 6' 9", and the only reason for it is that no one is blocking out. Everyone is just looking and waiting to see who can get the ball. Dave was probably a better rebounder and a better ballplayer because he didn't have very much natural jumping ability. He was a great athlete, but he knew he had to make himself better.

In a sense, we were all probably better back then because the game didn't come all that easily to us. The players today probably have more natural talent and get less out of it than we did fifteen and twenty years ago. They are such better athletes than we were that the game came very quickly to them, and so they've never bothered to learn the fundamentals of the sport. All the little skills of basketball are being lost because no one feels a need to focus on them anymore. Because the players can jump, they don't feel the need to box out. Because they can run, they don't feel the need to position their bodies correctly. Because they can dunk the ball, nobody works on the basic lay-up.

Of course, just because they have great natural athletic abilities doesn't make them ballplayers. A lot of the pros in the NBA today are just athletes impersonating basketball players. A basketball player is not just somebody who can jump and run. A player can also shoot the ball, he can dribble the ball, he can pass the ball, and he understands the game. Mark Jackson of the Knicks may not be the greatest of athletes, but he's a player. So is Larry Bird, even though he's slow and can't jump very well. But there aren't very many of them today.

I like Magic Johnson. He is a great, great player for

today's game, but only because no one tries to make him shoot from the outside. He's everybody's all-world, yet he can't shoot a fifteen-foot jump shot. Neither can Charles Barkley, and he's all-league, too. How many guys really can shoot from the outside today?

I think the overall level of pro basketball today has really fallen off. Once you get past the top four or five teams, the players simply aren't doing anything on the court except running up and down it. There seems to be no purpose in the movements of most teams' offenses. The players just move from spot to spot without much idea of why they're doing it. They aren't going anywhere. They pass the ball here and run over there and then they run to a spot. And then, after all that, they end up taking a twenty-five-foot jump shot. You don't need all that movement to wind up with a shot like that. The teams never seem to be saying, If your man does this, then we do that. They have movement, but they don't seem to have a plan.

There are too many teams and not enough talent. Expansion has hurt, and more expansion will hurt more. I admit it, there weren't very many good teams back when I played, either, but at least each team had some good players. Without enough pros who are fundamentally sound today, I think there are simply fewer good players. And there are no indications there will be more of them. Most of the players don't seem to want to work on their weaknesses today.

Maybe they feel they don't have to, with all their athletic ability. Maybe it's all the money they're making, but there don't seem to be any incentives for them to go that little extra step to make themselves better. The players today work on what they already can do, the way Cazzie used to practice his shooting.

Of course, the game has been changing for a long time now. When I played, the focus was on fundamentals, on pressure defense and boxing out. I think the changes started more or less around the time when the ABA, the old American Basketball Association, merged into the NBA. What happened then was sort of what took place when the old American Football League was absorbed into the NFL. The old NFL had been symbolized by the solid, no-fooling-around Green Bay Packers. Three yards and a cloud of dust. The AFL brought in speed and Joe Namath's flair and Hank Stram's flashy option offense of the seventies. It happened in baseball, too, around the same time, when Astroturf fields started replacing grass. The emphasis shifted to innate athletic ability. It didn't matter so much if you could catch the ball, or knew how to hit to the opposite field. Just as long as you could run or had some natural talent, you could play.

Throughout sports, and particularly in basketball, speed became the most important factor for a player. That's what the ABA emphasized: running and jumping and getting the ball upcourt quickly and then putting on the moves. I think the NBA was ripe for some changes and ready for what the ABA represented. Right around that time, Golden State won the NBA championship using the whole bench and running the court all the time. Then the ABA came in, and the transition to a speed, showtime-type of game really took off.

Dr. J and players like George Gervin and George McGinniss who were stars in the ABA were now stars in the NBA, and changed the style of play in the league. Coaches who had been in the ABA were now the NBA coaches, and they brought with them their concepts of speed and flair. Most of the coaches now believed they could win with just offense, and so do today's fans.

The coaches and the players know the fans go berserk when they see Michael Jordan flying through the air or Dominique Wilkins spinning and slamming. The crowd wants to see spectacular points when Michael and Dominique hook up. When I went against Earl Monroe, people would say, Hey, man, Frazier's not going to let him score those points. Oh, yeah, let's see if he can stop him.

So you give the fans what you think they want. Isiah Thomas in many ways is typical of today's NBA ballplayer. He's very good, make no mistake about that. I think he's an awesome talent. But I also think he's too showtimey now. He's got too much herky-jerky in his game, giving all these moves and fakes he doesn't need to do. He doesn't look serious out there to me, and I think sometimes he's just playing around. He looks like he's trying to see what fancy thing he can do. When he's on a break, it seems as if he's trying to think of something really spectacular to do so everyone will stand up and cheer.

Like Isiah, many of today's players have great talent, but many of them aren't reaching their potential. Instead, they remain one-dimensional players as the sport becomes a specialized game. Why isn't a guard a guard today and not a point guard or an off guard? Does that mean the second guard doesn't have to handle the ball? Well, I guess he doesn't, and can't. Why is there a power forward and a small forward? Does that mean the small forward has no power?

So many of the players on the pro level could be good ballplayers if only they had gotten the right coaching. They didn't get the advice and instruction in their formative years that I received, or Oscar Robertson or Jerry West got. Times have changed, everyone says. If I tell people how I was coached, the way I was brought up, they tell me that was then, this is now. I guess it is. A lot of times in high schools today, the coaches can't even make the kids runs laps. A kid will tell the coach, "I'm not going to run laps. What are you going to do about it?" And what is the coach going to do about it? Most of the coaches don't have the guts to just kick the kid off the team. How can the coaches enforce discipline on their teams if parents aren't doing it in their homes? I know times have changed in homes and in families, and I wish they hadn't.

It's probably up to the coaches to change the game, to bring it back to what it was, but they can't, and I'm sure they wouldn't even if they could. The new breed of coach isn't from the old school. When Red went back to coaching the Knicks in the late seventies, the game had already passed him by. The new type of player, who wasn't schooled in the fundamentals, was alien to him. He couldn't reach them. They didn't understand him and the kinds of things he wanted, or the way he wanted to play the game. They played a different brand of ball from what Red and I had known.

I'm not angry about how the game has changed. I accept the fact that it's the way people want it to be. I'm just glad I'm not playing now. It isn't my game anymore.

DeBusschere was the man we looked to for the key rebound down the stretch. He was probably better even than Willis at getting the ball, offensively or defensively, at that moment when we had to have it. And he could shoot, too. Dave could miss seven in a row, but when they counted, down the stretch, he hit them. He had incredible range on his shot, and sometimes I used to think he was better taking a thirty-footer than trying to make something from ten or fifteen feet.

From the beginning, DeBusschere fit right in with the Knicks. After just a couple of practices with the team, it was the Butcher who was putting in a lot of our offensive plays. While Red concentrated most of his time on the defense, it was Dave who first suggested the Barry play, because, he said, San Francisco had been so effective with it.

The trade for Dave, everybody has said, was the final piece of the puzzle. He was the missing link, and when he came to the Knicks, that completed the picture. The Knicks now had everything they needed, and began to mesh. But DeBusschere coming to New York also did something else, something everyone's forgotten but that also completed the puzzle. DeBusschere's arrival made me a starter.

I hadn't realized it myself, until that first time we played, when Red said, "You're the starter now." Hey, maybe it *really* wasn't such a bad trade after all. I know it changed my life. It was as if someone had pulled a veil from my eyes. All of a sudden, I found my offense. I started doing the things I had done in college. I began penetrating, and staying in the middle, dishing balls off or going for the hoop myself when I had the opportunity. Everything just seemed to snap into place, and for the first time in my pro career, I felt completely confident, not just defensively.

Two days after Dave broke his nose, we were playing the Warriors in San Francisco and DeBusschere was back, wearing a white mask that covered three-quarters of his face. There were layers of tape across his forehead and stretching from the bridge of his nose past his cheeks almost to his ears. He looked like a man from Mars.

"Hey, Butcher, you just fly in from some planet?" Barnett asked him in the locker room. "We your prisoners, or somethin'? You want me to take you to our captain?"

"I'll deal with the invader," Willis told him. "How much you want to spare all of us?"

With his mask and tape and all, the Butcher went out and played probably his best game of the season. He went up against Nate Thurmond, and Clyde Lee, and Jerry Lucas, and you could tell he was obviously in pain. I could see he wasn't breathing very well, and was trying to inhale through his mouth as he ran the court. I really didn't know how he could see the backboard, not to mention the hoop, but he was making just about everything he threw up. He hit the jumper and he even went under the basket and got sixteen rebounds. I guess Dave figured he had nothing to lose, with his nose broken already. He didn't have to worry anymore about getting it broken again. After the game, the Knicks' tenth win in a row, Barnett asked DeBusschere, "Hey, man, you got another one of those masks around?"

The season's record was now 15–1, the best start ever in the NBA. Of course, that was information I got from the newspapers and television. We didn't talk about it very much on the team. When you're on a winning streak, no one wants to bring it up. It's like in baseball when a pitcher is throwing a no-hitter. If we don't notice it, we can't jinx it. Still, I did notice that the guys were starting to wear the same clothes they had been wearing at earlier games. Red had on the same black suit and the same white shirt at every game. Nate was always playing the exact same jazz tape on his cassette player in the locker room before we went out on the court. I did change my clothes from game to game, but at each game I was starting to take off my shirt in exactly the same way, hanging it very precisely, just like I had done the last time. When I got dressed, I made sure to put the right shoe on first and then the left, never the other way around. When I went out on the court, without thinking very much about it, I made sure to shoot my free throws first, before I started taking any jump shots.

A few days after we flew home from the road trip, 250,000 people marched in Washington to protest the war in Vietnam. It was part of a nationwide wave of protests called the Vietnam Moratorium. Normally, I didn't read much more in the papers than the sports. But to get to the sports section, I had to pass by the front pages. Just picking up the *Daily News* or the *New York Post* made me a little aware of what was going on in the world. The headlines were always about guys getting killed, troops being shipped out, and those protests. And with television, too, you had to be completely out of it not to notice. Still, ballplayers live in a bubble, going from one game to the next practice to the game after that. Your whole life hinges on whether your shot is going in or why your shot isn't going in. For eight months of the year, that's all most of us think about: It's our business. But even in the off-season, you just can't take off and forget about what's been dominating your life. By the time you're starting to relax, it's time to get cranked up again. You feel the world's not changing too much, that you can drop out of it and pick it back up when you want, and things will be pretty much the same. It's not a good way to live, and today I regret that I didn't spend more time reading and finding out what was going on around me, but that's the way it was. If you spend all your time worrying about your jump shot, you just can't worry about the problems of the world as well.

However, if you're lucky enough to play in New York, the media capital, it's easier to see outside the players' bubble. And with intelligent, aware guys like Bradley and Phil Jackson around, in the locker room I'd frequently hear about somebody's buddy, some poor, unlucky stiff who got shipped out and never made it back.

I also made a point of reading about the war. I was interested because I had come so close to being in it. My rookie year, I was classified 1-A for the draft, most likely to be taken in and sent over there. I was scared. I went down to the draft board and showed them papers proving that I was the sole support of my mother and seven sisters—since my father wasn't around much—as well as, most important, my wife and my son.

Right before my junior year at SIU, when I would have to sit out from basketball for a year, I got married. Before then, there had always been two things I never wanted. I never wanted to go into the army and I never wanted to get married. I guess one out of two wasn't bad. Marsha was a year ahead of me at Southern Illinois. We used to study together, and she would help me with my classes. She was my only girlfriend in college. When I went off to school, I was too unsure of myself and too shy to talk to any girls, and didn't have a girlfriend for the entire first year. After Marsha and I met, we didn't see anybody else, and then, in the summer before my junior year, we married. Not much later, little Walt came along. When my son was born, it was the happiest moment of my life. I had desperately wanted a son—I guess every man does—but I just knew it would be a girl. The Fraziers are mostly women, my own immediate family, my uncle's, my grandparents'. I didn't think I had much chance. "If it's a girl," I told my wife, "you can name her." But on the off-chance it was a boy, he was going to be Walt Frazier III. And he is.

I became a family man and a more responsible person. We lived off-campus in a trailer, and weekends were family

time. If we could, the two of us might go out to the movies.
That was our entertainment. I couldn't hang out with the
guys the way I used to. Weekdays were for school and basketball. There wasn't much free time. It was a tough period.

The marriage lasted a year and a half. It was a rocky
time, and we had some pretty bad problems. I thought she
was overly jealous, and maybe I wasn't mature enough.
Maybe we were both too young. We divorced, which we had
to do, and she got custody of our son, which was right, but
not being able to have little Walt grow up with me around
all the time is one of the few things I regret in my life. After
the divorce, I used to have him with me during the summers,
for three months or so. Whatever has been important in his
life—when he graduated from high school, when he started
playing ball at the University of Pennsylvania—I was there.
Yet it isn't the same as being with him all the time. He's finishing off at Penn now, and although we are close, I still wish
I could have spent more time with him than I did. Even so,
I think he has a lot of me in him. He's so quiet and reserved,
sometimes you hardly know he's around. He never gave his
parents any problems, but he's never been motivated the
way I was. He's never been as disciplined as I was. Maybe if
I had spent more time with him, he would be.

Although the marriage didn't work, it did keep me out
of the army. The draft board reclassified me and I didn't
have to go to Vietnam, or even into the reserves like Cazzie

had to do. Once a month he might miss a game or two, and I would think, Man, am I fortunate. That could be me.

Back at the Garden, we were demolishing Cincinnati when Luther Rackley, a 6′ 10″ Royals rookie, started pushing Willis. He gave the captain one big shove under the Knick basket, and Willis decided he wasn't going to take any more of it. He pulled back that huge hand and smashed Rackley in the face with an overhand right. *Bong.* Rackley was down, and out. His nose looked broken.

I was happy. I didn't like Rackley. He was a dirty player, and I think he got what was coming to him. Except for this time with Willis, he usually picked on the little guys. He was the kind of player who always tried to rough you up when you cut by him just because he was bigger than you. He had already done it to me a few times, pushing me around, getting in an extra shove any time he had the chance. He was arrogant, and I thought he got what he deserved.

Rackley wasn't the only player like that in the league. The NBA was a lot tougher then than it is now because just about every team had one guy whose job wasn't just to play ball but also to be an enforcer. He would push the other team around and make sure his own teammates didn't get pushed back too much. We had players like the Pistons' Reggie Harding, who, word had it, used to carry a gun around. A few years after he left the league, Harding was shot and killed on the streets of Detroit. The players were tough off the court and didn't change much when they put on their uniforms to play ball. John Tresvant, Bill Bridges, Joe Strawder—man, these were pugnacious guys, guys who didn't care too much if you got hurt. That was the price you paid. One of the players you really had to watch out for was Atlanta's Walt Hazzard. I saw a lot of times that when you went in for a lay-up against Hazzard, he'd try to undercut the man. He'd come up beneath you when you were in the air, and you can really get hurt that way. I knew when I went in against him or Joe Strawder that I had to protect myself and look down as well as up when I was shooting.

The league also was tougher then because hand checking was allowed. You spend three quarters of a game with someone's hand always on your hip, you keep trying to smack it away, and he keeps putting it back, and finally, you've had enough. All of a sudden, it comes to a head and there's a fight. Today, you can't hand check, which is maybe one of the reasons there are fewer fights—and why the defense isn't as good. I think the rule banning hand checking was put in because the NBA realized there are a lot of guys today who can't shoot the ball and the league wanted to protect them and to encourage a more crowd-pleasing, up-and-down style of play. If you had hand checking today, there would be some players, even stars like Magic Johnson and Buck Williams, who'd have great difficulty scoring. With a hand on their hip, you could keep them away from the basket, and if they can't get to the hoop, they're not a real threat without an outside shot.

Magic's a great ballhandler and passer, the best I've ever seen leading the break, but what can Magic do to you if he can't drive? All you have to do is watch him for a few minutes and it's obvious. He can only shoot going to his right. He has to get set. He doesn't really jump much on his shot. Yet today's players act as if he's really dangerous out there, and they go out and guard Magic on the perimeter. So of course he gets by them and he is very, very dangerous, a 6′ 9″ Earl Monroe, once he penetrates to the basket.

When Magic has the ball upcourt, I wouldn't be interested in what he was doing. I would stay off him, cutting off his drive, and force him to shoot from the outside, not just taking that shot when he wants to. Hey, Magic, beat me outside. If he can do it, hitting twenty-foot jumpers, I could live with that. But I still really wouldn't worry about him until he got down near the free-throw line. Magic is too good to have the advantage of everybody letting him do exactly what he wants to do.

But that's how everybody seems to play defense today. I watch the Lakers against the Celtics and I don't see James Worthy even one time go to his left. Kevin McHale will be guarding him and then Larry Bird, and not once during a game will they force Worthy away from his right and from what he does best. When I see that kind of thing, I know there can't be any kind of real defensive strategy in the game, no real coaching going on.

It's not just against the Lakers and against Magic and Worthy. Watch Bird. How many players make him drive? Every time I see Bird, he's standing out there and taking an uncontested jump shot. He's a great outside shooter, so it makes sense that you have to force him to drive. Make him do something he doesn't want to do. Make that his first option. The way I'd play Bird would be first to get up real tight on him, so he couldn't get the outside shot off. Normally, with a right-handed player like Bird, I'd want to force him to drive to his left. But because he has such good court awareness and peripheral vision, even going left, he could still hit his teammates. So I'd start him going right, and then force him to his left, where he wouldn't be able to see guys coming over to help out.

I've always believed that the 1970 Knicks, even though they'd be much smaller than most of the teams today, could play with any of them because we played defense. That would keep us in it. We played intelligent defense and knew how to take advantage of what the other team gave us. In our day, a player like Magic would have hurt Kareem, because he would have allowed us to collapse on the middle. That doesn't mean we would have all left our positions and given Magic clear passing lanes. But we'd always be ready to help out, and not give up the open shot. I think we'd be able to at least neutralize today's best players, like Magic and Bird and Dominique Wilkins. The one player today who would give us the most trouble is Michael Jordan. He doesn't really have a noticeable weakness. All you can do with him is first dare him to try to beat you from the outside. If he's hitting from there, you'd have to take a chance with the other players on his team, double on Michael and see if *they* could beat you. He's a terrific player who can do everything now, but I wonder as his teams get better and better if he'll be able to adjust to playing a smaller role and scoring less. Will he be just as happy when he's scoring 25 instead of 35? How will he react when he's taking only twenty shots a game instead of thirty?

I think on offense, the '70 Knicks would find it pretty easy to score today. I think a lot of the old players would score a lot more points today, because without real defense, it's so much easier to put it in the hoop. It's extremely rare today for a team to pick up from end line to end line. Nobody even pressures very much at half court anymore. If a man meets you at the half-court line, he backs up until he gets to the area of the free-throw line extended. That's when today's players finally start to apply pressure.

We'd know how to take advantage of a team's defensive problems. Consider Larry Bird again. As great as he is, on defense he's a liability. He plays what I call "matador defense," waving at the other team as they go by him. He doesn't really guard anyone, because he knows he doesn't have the foot speed, so when his man gets the ball, he is constantly backing up, afraid the guy is going to go around him. Bird's always on a lesser player, the guy who has no jump shot, and the other teams don't seem to be smart enough to take advantage of his inadequacies on defense. Because Bird's smart, and the Celtics, unlike most other teams, play a kind of team defense, he gets away with it. I don't think he would against us.

When Willis punched Luther Rackley out, it was a fight between two blacks, but most fights in the NBA then—and now—were usually between blacks and whites. There were some real tough white players, not patsies at all, but a lot of blacks think the whites won't fight back, so they feel they don't have much to lose if they start throwing punches. If they see a brother, they're not as likely to start a fight as quickly because they're pretty sure punches will come back at them. If a guy knows someone can hit him and rearrange his face, it makes him think twice. He'll push and shove, but when it comes right down to it, he'll hold back from fighting.

Rackley obviously picked on the wrong guy. Even before I had gotten into the league, I had heard the story about how Willis took out the entire Laker team, starting with Rudy LaRusso, and then just flattened one after another as they came at him. I saw him punch out the Hawks, too, one time down in Atlanta. Nate Bowman tried to grab him at one point, to stop the bloodshed, and Willis knocked him down, too. Nate meant well, but that was the worst thing to do when Willis got angry. When he started fighting, he would look for a wall, get his back against it—so nobody could jump him from behind—and then if anybody approached him, he'd swat the guy away.

On November 26, the day before Thanksgiving, we carried a 21–1 record and 16 wins in a row down to Atlanta to play the Hawks. Another victory would tie the NBA record for the most consecutive wins. I wasn't too focused on that possibility, however, because I had more important things to deal with. I had to get me some tickets.

For my sisters and brother and mother and relatives and friends, I figured out that I needed seventeen tickets for the game at Alexander Coliseum. Normally, each player got two tickets for a road game, but I had started working on this one early. I had told Red in New York that I'd need extra tickets in Atlanta, and he got me some. Danny Whelan got me a few. I picked up some more from Riordan and Bradley and John Warren, who weren't using theirs. They knew that when we went to California, they could have my tickets out there. It was a hot game, a sellout, so most of the guys had already used their tickets. I still needed about seven more seats, and I had to buy them. Unlike most athletes, I wasn't completely adverse to paying for them out of my own pocket.

In a way, I sort of dreaded going to Atlanta. Even though I might not show it, I was almost bashful on the court. I never liked looking up into the stands and seeing people there. If I didn't know anyone was there, I could imagine I was alone and much more easily go out and play. If I don't know anyone's there and no one knows me, I can perform. I can be anonymous, which I like. But in Atlanta, I knew damn well my family and friends were there and they'd be watching every move I made. My feelings about returning home had always been a little ambiguous. It was good, of course, to see my family. But I also had to do so much running around, getting tickets and seeing people. I had to go to my mother's and eat so she could serve me a gigantic meal. I had to see all the family and a lot of old friends. It was exhausting, happy, and difficult all at once. I never got any rest. Any other city, I could just go to my hotel room, take the phone off the hook, switch on the TV, and lie down. Not in Atlanta.

Our plane got into Atlanta near two o'clock in the morning. We went directly to the hotel, and I sacked out. When I got up the next morning, the first thing I did was to call my mom. My mother was a confident, aggressive, and very tough lady. When my father wasn't there, it was Eula Frazier who inspired us, who advised us, who taught us about not dishonoring the family name. She always told me, whatever I did, just try to be the best. My mother was the family's emotional support, our base. I got my big eyes from her, and my confidence.

I called her and told her what I wanted to eat. I wasn't yet into soy milk and nutty granola, and she never was. I told her I wanted some steamed collard greens with pork, carrots, and, of course, her fried chicken. She made terrific fried chicken. I got over to the house around twelve-thirty, and almost the whole family was waiting there for me. Except for my father, of course. When I walked in, at first my sisters didn't know what to call me. To most of them, I had always been June, because I'm really Walt Frazier, Jr. But now they had been reading in the papers that I was known as Clyde, and I was a different kind of person from the quiet boy they had known. To my mom, though, I was still Walt, which she had always called me, and I was still the same to her. "You know," she said after I'd been there a bit, "you're no different than you used to be."

As usual, the meal was enormous. My mother ran around her little kitchen and just kept bringing out more and more food. I watched her rushing in and out and I remembered how when I was growing up, when friends would get a new house, she always talked about wanting one herself. A new house with a big kitchen. As a kid, I used to pray to God, Please, God, let me be a good player so I can make some money and buy my mom a house. A house with an absolutely humongous kitchen.

In 1972, I called my mom up one morning and told her, "I got the money now. Go out and buy any house you like. Buy yourself what you've always wanted." A month later, she still hadn't found a house to buy. After all the years without too much money, now she couldn't accept spending so much all at one time. To just go ahead and put down fifty thousand dollars like that was beyond her ability to imagine. So I came down from New York and found the house in a week. Naturally, it had a big kitchen, and also a swimming pool. It was in southwest Atlanta, in the neighborhood where Andy Young and Maynard Jackson lived. My sisters were angry about the house. They thought it was too far out from downtown. At night, there were rabbits running around in the backyard, and they thought it was too rural. They were afraid of the darkness and the quiet, and so for two weeks they would not go out there. Finally, they all moved in, and my dream was fulfilled. Everything else has been icing on the cake. I had reached my goal. I had done what I had always wanted to do for my mother. It didn't matter if I won championships, and I didn't care about any awards. For years, my sole inspiration had been to get my mother that house, and I had done it. Nothing could, and nothing can, compare to it.

The funny thing was, my mother and I were actually

friendly enemies while I was growing up. When I was younger, I got a lot of whippings from her, because when she'd leave the house, I was supposed to watch the younger kids. Instead, I'd go down to the playground to play some ball. When I got older, I thought she drank too much and smoked too much and I would try to tell her to stop, or at least cut down. Somehow, we always wound up in an argument. I don't think she understood that I was trying to give back to her what she had given to me, the discipline and the pride, and the knowledge that you always had to work hard for what you wanted.

A few years ago, I was being honored in Norfolk, Virginia, when I got a phone call in my hotel room telling me my mother had passed away, at the age of fifty-six. I don't remember hanging up the phone. I don't know if I dropped it, or what. I lay down in bed and didn't want to move. I wanted to stay in that room forever. I felt emptier than I ever had or can imagine I ever will again. Even now, there are few days I don't think of her. At least, I tell myself, I got her that house when I did, with that big kitchen.

After stuffing myself with the fried chicken, I finally got ready to leave my mother's house and go to the game. I was bloated and lethargic, and as I walked out the door, my mother called after me, "Walt, don't you let those Hawks beat you." The way I was feeling, that was all I needed to hear.

My mother never saw me play basketball in high school, or when I was in college. Until I played for the Knicks, she had never seen a basketball game. She only saw me play football because one of my sisters was a majorette, and she came to watch her. But when I became a professional, she became a fanatical fan. She never missed a game whenever we played in Atlanta. Sitting in the stands surrounded by her children, she'd always make herself known. I couldn't hear her from the court, but everybody else could. People would tell me later, "Hey, I heard your momma at the game. She was really laying it out." "That's my son!" my mom would shout. "That's my son," whenever I did something good.

I didn't think she was going to have much to shout about tonight. When we stepped on the court, the P.A. announcer told the crowd that the Knicks have won sixteen in a row, and I said to myself, maybe for the first time, Man, sixteen in a row. That's something. It's exciting, but for most of the game, I didn't play excited. I felt like my legs were made of cement and they were so heavy I could barely lift them. The Hawks were always a tough team to play, very physical and probably the dirtiest team in the league, and they seemed on top of us all night. Up until the third quarter, nothing much happened in the game. Both teams went up and down the court with neither club gaining much of an advantage. Then, suddenly, it was as if somebody turned the electricity on.

DeBusschere intercepted a pass, threw it upcourt to me,

I got fouled and I made the two free throws. Then Barnett intercepted and scored. Now it was Bradley's turn. He took the ball away from Lou Hudson, fed me, and I scored on another lay-up. The Hawks couldn't bring the ball up.

We could taste blood now.

We saw it in their eyes. They didn't know what was happening to them. They were professionals, and they couldn't get the damn ball up the court. They were looking around at each other, waiting for one of them to do something, anything, that was going to stop what was happening to them.

Bradley took the ball away from Hazzard this time, and I got another lay-up. After being up by 7 at the half, we were leading now by more than 20, and it wasn't over yet. Hazzard tried to dribble down the right side, and I poked it away from him for another lay-up. Then he tried it down the left sideline and I popped it out of his hands, and once again, I was gone. One more time, the third in a row, I got him, coming around from the back side, flicking at the ball, and it was mine, another lay-up.

I had been tired to begin with, and now I was exhausted, after running up and down the court so many times all by myself. While the Hawks were trying to take the ball out after the last lay-up, I ran back up the court past Lou Hudson and told him, "Hey, man, hold on to the damn ball, will you? I'm beat, man. Hold on to it now and gimme a break."

Not just me but the whole team was in an almost perfect

groove. We scored 14 straight points and then, after a Hawk basket, 12 more in a row. I don't ever remember ten or twelve minutes of basketball as perfect as these. For this one quarter in Atlanta, we played basketball as well as it can be played. We outscored the Hawks, who were leading their division, by 38 to 12. At the end of the quarter, the game was over. We tied the record for most consecutive wins.

Afterward, outside the locker room, my mother told me that she was very proud that I played a good game.

We went for the record in Cleveland, against Cincinnati, not one of the league's better teams. Before the game, there were newspaper reporters and magazine writers and microphones everywhere. But Red had his rules, and no one got in the locker room. No one was allowed to bother us before the game. The room was quiet, no one mentioning the record or even saying anything about the streak. No one had to. We all knew very well that we were trying to break a record that had lasted for a quarter of a century.

We didn't play much like we knew, or cared, for most of the game. We seemed out of sync. Only Cazzie, who came off the bench in the second quarter, kept us close. And while we were lethargic, Oscar Robertson wasn't. The Big O wasn't selfish, but if he had been, he would have set records no other guard would ever approach. He never was out of control. As always, he took the shot he wanted to take, not the shot I'd let him have. When I had him ten feet from the basket, he tried to get five feet away. When I had him five feet out, he wanted a lay-up. I was in his jock, staying right in front of him, but he was so strong and physical, he was beating the hell out of me and moving me around where he wanted to go. He was 6′ 5″ and probably around 220, and that kind of size should be outlawed for a guard. It was impossible to get around and steal the ball from him, he was so big and bulky and strong. And you couldn't block his shot, either. He'd get the ball all the way back when he went up, and I just couldn't reach it. My chest was starting to hurt.

The Royals were up by three with under two minutes to go when Oscar fouled out. Thank God, I said to myself.

The coach of the Royals was Bob Cousy, who was over forty years old. A couple of days before, Cousy had put himself on the active list, but hadn't yet played a second in this game. Instead of getting off his bench a player who was really in shape, he put himself in. I was ticked off. He's hot-dogging it, I thought. There was no reason for him to enter the game now, except that he felt it was over and he could come in and get some of the glory for beating us and breaking the streak. We had all busted our butts for forty minutes, and here he was trying to take some of the credit for it. He walked onto the court in such an arrogant way, like he was still the king of basketball, and it got me even angrier.

At first, though, he surprised me. He threw a good pass

to Norm Van Lier for a jumper and then made two free throws himself to give the Royals a 105–100 lead. There were twenty-six seconds left in the game.

It was over. I knew it was over. Ballplayers never say die, right? Like hell they don't. The streak was gone, and I knew it. Maybe we could start a new one next game.

Rich got a nice pass into Willis, who missed the shot but got fouled when he tried to follow it. Reed made the two free throws and it was now 105–102, sixteen seconds to go. Red was screaming, "Go out, see the ball, get up on them, double them." We were not even thinking now, just reacting. More from instinct than anything else, we played tough defense on the in-bounds pass. Bradley jumped up and down and Van Lier couldn't get it in, so they called a time out. It was their last.

By the bench, Red reminded us, "Press them, press them. Double up. Don't worry about them getting past you."

The Royals tried to in-bounds it again, and this time it was Cousy who was going to try to throw the ball in. What arrogance! I windmilled my arms all over to try to block his sight. He was looking to be clever and wanted to hit Connie Dierking, the Royals center and the last guy you'd expect to get the pass. But Willis was all over him. We were covering everybody tightly, and Cousy looked desperate. Finally, with no more time-outs left, he tried to get the ball out to Tom

Van Arsdale. Dave saw the pass coming all the way, cut in front of Van Arsdale, and raced down the court for a slam. 105–104. Thirteen seconds left.

It had been over, but it wasn't over now. As soon as Dave grabbed the ball, I knew we could pull it out. We could do it.

It was Cousy again taking the ball out. He passed it in to Van Arsdale on the right side, and DeBusschere was there again, right on top of him. Van Arsdale moved up the sideline when Mike Riordan came over to double on him. Van Arsdale tried to dribble out of the trap, but Willis came up and deflected the ball away. It was right there, bouncing in front of me. I grabbed it and dribbled a couple of times, heading toward the Royals' basket. Out of the corner of my eye, I saw Dave wide open and cutting to the basket, but I didn't know whether he could get the shot off before the buzzer sounded. I didn't know how much time was left, so when I got to the top of the key, I threw up a running jumper. I was a little out of control, and so the shot hit the back of the rim. Incredibly, it bounced over the head of Van Arsdale and right back to me. I went up for the rebound and I knew that time was running out, so I didn't come down. I shot it again from the air, and missed again, but Van Arsdale's momentum carried him into me a little. There was no doubt about it; the referee called a foul.

I lay on the floor, saying to myself, God, why didn't that ball go in? My job would've been over. I looked up at the clock to see how much time was left, but it didn't matter now. There were two seconds to go. The Royals were over the limit, and I had three chances to make two. Three shots. The worst I could do was make one, and the game is tied, that was the absolute worst thing that could happen. Well, I guessed the worst was that I could miss all three and then have to go into the Royals' locker room. I'd be welcome there. I couldn't go back to the Knicks' room after that.

Normally, I thrive on pressure. The greater the pressure, the more relaxed I am. Pressure helps me concentrate. But now, right now, I really didn't want to go to the line in a situation like this. It looked like a no-win situation. I was expected to make the shots. All I could do was disappoint everybody. I walked to the line thinking that I looked calm, but inside my heart was beating like a jackhammer. I wasn't sweating, 'cause I don't sweat very much in general, but my body felt tight. My knees were a little weak. I was very excited.

Red called out, "Relax, Clyde, take your time." Willis told me, "You can do it man, no sweat."

I was a situational free-throw shooter. Sometimes I was terrible, and I felt like my feet were embedded in mud when I went to the line. No matter what I'd do, no matter how many times I would bounce the ball, I could never seem to get comfortable. I seldom missed a crucial free throw, though. I saw the important free throws as money. Hey, this is cash right here. If I miss this sucker, I'm throwing away good money.

I came to the spot, put my right foot close to the line and my left foot off to the side. I tried to remember what all little kids are taught about free-throw shooting: elbows straight. Put an arc on the ball. Take a deep breath and shake the tension off. I bounced the ball three times with the left hand and then put it in my right hand. I held the ball on the seams, away from the label. I focused on the back of the rim and went straight up, without a pause. It didn't touch anything but the bottom of the net. The score was tied.

That was it. There was no more pressure. If I had missed the first one, I would have been uptight, but now I didn't have to worry. The least I'd done was tied the game. Now I was confident. I dribbled three more times, sighted the back of the rim, and put the second dead away.

It was over, even though there were still two seconds left on the clock. Cousy in-bounded one last time, and I saw Reed intercept again. But instead of just holding on to the ball, Willis tried to go up for a shot and almost banged into Van Lier as the clock ran out. For a split-second, I expected the refs to call a charging foul on him and we'd have been dead. There was no call. The Knicks won 106–105, for our eighteenth consecutive victory, a new NBA record.

We ran into the locker room jumping and screaming, like we were junior high school kids who had just won the championship of the neighborhood. Everything that we had been holding in for so long came out now. The Rave was raving. Cazzie announced, in his radio broadcaster's voice, that "The Knickerbockers of New York City have, ladies and gentlemen, just set an all-time record." Bradley and Barnett slapped palms, somebody handed me a bottle of Scotch, which I don't drink, and I just stared at it, with a dumb look on my face.

That night, I broke two rules I usually adhered to. I partied on the road, and I hung out with my teammates. With Barnett and Bowman and some of the others, we hit a Cleveland nightclub and celebrated together. The pressure was off.

The next night, we were back at the Garden, against the Pistons, and the air was out of the balloon. We had been to the peak of the mountain and there was nothing left, nothing to do but come down from the heights. We were professionals and we approached the game just like any other, but it wasn't there, and we all knew it from the beginning. We dropped behind early and couldn't do anything to get back in it. We made a run early in the fourth quarter, but that

was all we had. With less than a minute to go, we were completely out of it when all the fans in the Garden got up and
started giving us a standing ovation. I got goose bumps. Fans
cheer for a good play or sometimes for a good game. But
this time they were cheering for something we hadn't even
been doing this night.

In the locker room, we all sat pretty quietly in front of
our cubicles when Red came in. "You guys stink," he said
with a smile on his face. "Tomorrow you're all off, do whatever you want to do. Tonight, all of you just go out and have
a good time."

CHAPTER

6

THE REGULAR SEASON WAS OVER. NO ONE SAID IT, no one acted or played like they didn't have to put out anymore, but in some way, I think, we all knew it. It was only the month of December, and everybody on the team kept saying to one another and to the press that there was a long way to go yet. Physically, we didn't intentionally let up, or try to pace ourselves. We still wanted to win, and Red still reminded us all the time that "leads can be blown," and we all nodded our heads and agreed. The season was only less than a third over. Still, our record was 23–2, and when I looked at the standings in the papers and saw how far the Bullets and Bucks were behind, I figured there was no way anybody could catch us. Hey, we'd really have to be terrible to blow it now.

We were almost never terrible, at least not for very long, and almost always managed to win when we had to and to stay far enough ahead of the teams chasing us. After the Pistons ended the winning streak, we immediately won three more in a row, including a romp over the Sonics at the Garden. In the third quarter, we outscored them by 30 even though I kept missing my free throws. It was one of those nights when I couldn't get comfortable at the line and when the ball just didn't feel right in my hands. With the subs playing most of the fourth quarter, I sat on the bench next to Willis, who was not going to let me forget what I'd been doing on the line.

"Hey, man, I don't know how you could have made those ones out in Cleveland last week. This here tonight, my man, this is the real you. You were just lucky last time out."

When I came into the locker room, there was the ugliest hat in the world on the seat in front of my locker. Oh, yeah, I thought, I'm getting the hat trick, just because I missed three free throws in a row. It had to be Barnett who set this up. Not only did it look like one of Rich's hats, it was also the kind of joke he would pull. Only people who have experience in practical jokes should do them. I tried it once, when we had a guy named Tom Riker playing for the Knicks. He was a big guy who was a terrible free-throw shooter. After he had missed a lot of them during a game, I threw my hat, a real nice one, at him in the locker room. "Hey, man, you got the hat trick," I said. The guy didn't laugh. He stomped right on my good hat. Last time I ever played that trick. My hats were too expensive.

Although for the rest of the regular season we never

played as well for a stretch as we had during the streak, eighteen in a row had made the Knicks the fashionable team to follow. We stayed that way, being shown on national TV almost every time the league had a game televised. We weren't dumb about it. There was money to be made, we realized, and this was the time to cash in. Only Willis, I think, had any incentive clauses in his contract for how many games we won and how well the team did. For the rest of us, it didn't matter if we won every game the entire season, it wasn't going to add anything to our paychecks. We had to get any extra money where we could, and on our own. Bradley was the only one who didn't take advantage and try to cash in. Maybe he was already thinking of his political career, but he refused to do any commercials or make any endorsements. That's his business, I thought. Not mine.

One day my agent got a call from Ben Khan, a famous New York furrier. Would I be interested in a fur coat in exchange for doing some advertising? I would be very interested, and I got a full-length seal coat for my interest. Some of the guys, including me, signed book contracts to write about the Knicks. Together as a team—that is, without Bradley—we did a Vitalis commercial, with everybody sharing in the revenue. There were personal appearances, going to shopping malls, signing autographs, clinics, posing for magazine covers.

"Hey, Clyde, will you sign, 'To my best friend, Jimmy'?"

"Clyde, you got any extra clothes you can give me?"

"What's Willis really like? Is he as tough as they say?"

"Why doesn't Cazzie Russell start instead of Bill Bradley?"

I did as much of the stuff as I could. With the exception of Bill and Cazzie, who had signed big contracts when they came into the league, even though we weren't exactly starving, we weren't millionaires, either. Unlike the two of them, I didn't have a celebrity name coming out of college.

SIU was small college. No matter how well I played, my name still wasn't there in the big newspapers. It was just the way it was in Atlanta. When I read a sports record book, we weren't listed, and neither were teams we played like Kentucky Wesleyan and Evansville. They were good teams, but they were small college, too. I knew I was a good player, but I never thought I was good enough to be a pro ballplayer. Until near the end of my sophomore year, I never even thought about the possibility of pro ball. Then, at a late-season game, Earl Lloyd, who was a black scout for the Pistons, came down to watch us play. There was a big write-up in the school newspaper about him, and he was quoted as saying that he believed I had great potential as a pro player. For the first time, I thought, Maybe I could make a living at this game. Maybe I had a chance. The following spring, George McNeil, the guard I played behind at the beginning of the year, got drafted in the eighth round. Hey, I thought, the pros really must know about our school. Wow. Maybe, someday, if I was lucky, I could also get drafted in the eighth round.

When Southern Illinois won the NIT in my junior year, I knew that people outside of Carbondale had started to hear of me. Before the draft, I got feelers from Detroit and Chicago. The Bulls offered me twelve thousand dollars and the Pistons about the same. The average salary in the NBA in those days was somewhere around $16,000–$18,000. Jim Zimmerman, a lawyer who was advising me, asked the Bulls, "Well, what about a signing bonus?" "That's in there already," they told him. Because of sitting out my junior year, I had one more season of eligibility left, so Jim told the Bulls and the Pistons to forget it. I was going to go back to school. I wanted to play in the NBA, and I would have played for free, just to get a chance to prove myself; but if I was going to get paid, I wanted to be paid as much as possible.

When the Knicks, who had never contacted me at all before the draft, took me on the first round, they offered me a salary of twenty-five thousand dollars with a signing bonus of another twenty-five thousand. Jim told me the numbers and I said, Yeah, why not? That sounded like real money. I had no idea what I was worth, but the Knicks' offer sounded almost too good to believe. I went to class after talking to Jim and I could barely concentrate. My mind was gone. I couldn't hear the teacher. I couldn't study. All I could think of was pro ball, and how much they'd be paying me to play it.

Today, first-round draft choices routinely get a million and more a year. The best salary year I ever had, near the end of my career and after almost ten years as an all-star in the NBA, I got $350,000. It sounds like a lot, but a couple of seasons later, I was out of the league, at the age of thirty-four.

When the money did come in, I didn't spend it wildly, or at least I didn't think I went wild. I had only two vices, my family and clothes. My first responsibility, I felt, was to take care of my relatives. After that, I took care of myself. I constantly bought new suits, and there wasn't a week that went by when my tailor didn't have a new suit for me on the mannequin. Some months, I spent maybe twenty-five hundred, or even three thousand dollars on clothes. Sharkskin suits and alligator shoes weren't cheap. I didn't smoke, I didn't drink too much. Clothes were my pleasure.

When I first came to the Knicks and wasn't playing too much, or playing the way I thought I could, shopping made me happy. I bought something new every day, even if it was only a handkerchief. It made me feel better about myself. That first season had been a tough year. I turned my ankle real bad during the preseason and had to go on the injured list. I missed all the exhibitions and then had to sit out five games into the regular season. Even if I hadn't fallen behind, the adjustment would've been rough. In college ball, you got a tough guy to play against maybe every three games. In the pros, every night there was someone who could score points on you, and could stop you, too. If you got past him, you had to deal with someone else, someone 6′ 8″ or 6′ 9″, who was capable of blocking your shot. In the pros, the other players would come over to help out and you had to beat two or three men to score.

It was also tough being a rookie, because the older players would dump on you. Whenever we practiced, I had to carry the balls, and when we watched game films, I had to carry the projector. We were the low men on the totem pole. When the team went out on the road, the veterans would take the rookies' tickets. We'd get to Chicago, and Willis would say to me, "Hey, man, you don't want your tickets, do you?"

"No, Willis, I don't want any." What else could I say? Afterward, he just took my tickets, as a matter of course. If I wanted tickets from then on in Chicago, or Detroit, or Los Angeles, I had to purchase them.

I think that's different today. When a guy like Patrick Ewing comes out of college to the Knicks, he starts out as the star of the team. He has no experience, but the other players are already looking up to him. He's a young guy, but who's going to guide him around? Who would have the nerve to take him under their wing, the way Willis did with me? Nobody. Maybe that's one of the reasons so many players today are having problems with drugs. There's nobody on the team they respect who'll tell them what to do and what not to do. When I was a rookie, if the older guys saw the young players doing anything negative, they'd come right over and tell them. They knew that anything that would hurt the team would hurt their money, and so they were right on our butts. "Hey, man," Willis would tell me all the time, "don't stay out too late tonight. We got a game tomorrow. You got to get your sleep."

Willis and some of the others understood that there was so much more freedom in the pros than in college, and that was also a problem for me. In a sense, I guess, it should have made pro life easier. In college, I had to worry about making grades and attending classes. I had to study. In the pros, my only job was basketball. That was all I had to worry about, just maintaining my body and being ready to play. Before I came to the Knicks, I had always been under the thumbs of strict coaches, who ran their players' lives as much as they ran the basketball games. Under those coaches, we always did everything as a team. We ate together, we traveled together, we partied together. Now I was twenty-two years old and out on my own. I had to learn when to eat by myself and when not to eat, so I wouldn't be too full at game time.

I had to get to practice by myself and learn what to do with all my spare time.

Early in my rookie year, I was glad that I had signed a three-year contract, because I didn't think I would last three years. With Barnett and Howie Komives starting at the guards, I was coming off the bench to apply defensive pressure. Whoever was hot, my role was to stop him. With my defensive background at SIU, I had confidence I could stop anybody. But once, early on, Hal Greer of the Sixers must have beaten me three or four straight times down the floor, going by me like I wasn't even there. Nothing I tried against him worked, and he fouled me out in no time. That night, in my room, I cried. How was I going to be able to stay in this league?

Then, little by little, I started to hold my own defensively. I seemed to be able to concentrate more and became more comfortable on the court, at least defensively. I started to do some good things, stealing the ball from established players like Lou Hudson and Oscar Robertson and Jerry West. I started to think that I wasn't too far off from becoming a good player. With some hard work in the summer, with running and lifting weights, I thought I could become better, good enough at least to stay in the league.

As I started playing more and playing better, and as the team started to win a little more, I felt more comfortable about dressing up in my clothes and going out. Early on, when things had been bad, I had stayed in my room, got all dressed up, and just stared at myself in the mirror. I was awed by the city as much as I had been awed by pro ball. I couldn't believe all the channels you could find on television in New York. Sometimes I would leave my hotel room just to walk around and look at all the pretty women and all the people. It was like I was back in high school, where all the guys would hang out and I'd go home alone. I didn't know a soul in New York and didn't know where to go.

When things started to get better on the court, I started wishing I knew the New York scene like some of my teammates who were so comfortable in it. I used to hear Emmette Bryant and Freddie Crawford talking about the fun they had, and the places they went to. Man, did you hear about what went down at Small's Paradise? That's the place to go.

I gathered up my confidence and one night went up to Small's by myself. Atlanta had been an early town, with most everything closed up by around 1:00 A.M. If you wanted to do anything, you had to get moving by nine at night, which is when I got to Small's. There was no one there. Just me, looking around and trying not to appear too out of it. I hung around until eleven-thirty, surrounded by silence and empty tables. Hey, man, this is dead, what am I doing here? So I finally left and went home. The next day at practice, Freddie started talking about what a helluva time the guys had last night.

"Oh, where'd you all go?"

"Small's."

"You did? What time was that?"

"Oh, we got there about two-thirty or so."

It took time for me to adjust to New York, and to New Yorkers. I was becoming a celebrity, and when I walked from the hotel to the Garden for a game, people were starting to stop me on the street and ask how I was doing.

"Feeling good, feeling good," I'd tell them. So many people seemed to care that I started to think New Yorkers weren't like their reputation. They weren't as cold as people said, and were really concerned about how I felt, not just about basketball.

"Sucker," Barnett told me later. "They're not interested in your health. This is the garment district here, and those guys, they're gamblers. They want to know what kind of shape you in for the game tonight. Whether you are ready to play. They gotta know where to lay their money."

With the team winning, I was going out more and more. Winning makes the music sound better, the food taste better, and made me realize I liked people more than I thought. I had started the season as Walt Frazier, just a basketball player. Now I was becoming Clyde, kind of a man-about-town. I was mingling, talking to lots of different people in bars and clubs. And, surprise, enjoying it. After another win, I'd make a point of stopping off at the Harry M. club downstairs in the Garden. A lot of the guys did, but they always sat in the back, where the fans couldn't see them very well or get to them. Reed, DeBusschere, Barnett, and Bradley all liked to isolate themselves from the fans. I always hung around the front of the bar, where people could come over and buy me a drink if they wanted. I had different attitudes about going out than they did. When I hung out with any of the guys from the team, I was always ready to go, hit another place, when they were still happy to stay where they were. It was awkward, so I hardly ever saw my teammates once I left the locker room.

After leaving the Garden, I'd hit some place for dinner. I always ate out. Every day, every meal. I think I went seven straight years without eating at home. It seems incredible to me now. I only kept water in my refrigerator, even when I left the hotel and had my own place on the East Side. I don't think I ever turned the stove on. What was the point? I never cooked anything.

After eating, I made the rounds of my clubs: Studio 54, Le Club, Maxwell's Plum, Small's to finish off. I'd hit seven or eight places during the night, and because I was a cordial guy, I accepted drinks from anybody I met in all the places. A couple of times, somebody in Knick management told me

This was my game—stealing the ball. I got more pleasure from a steal than from a basket or a good pass. With steals, I could try to control the game at both ends. (Photo by George Kalinsky)

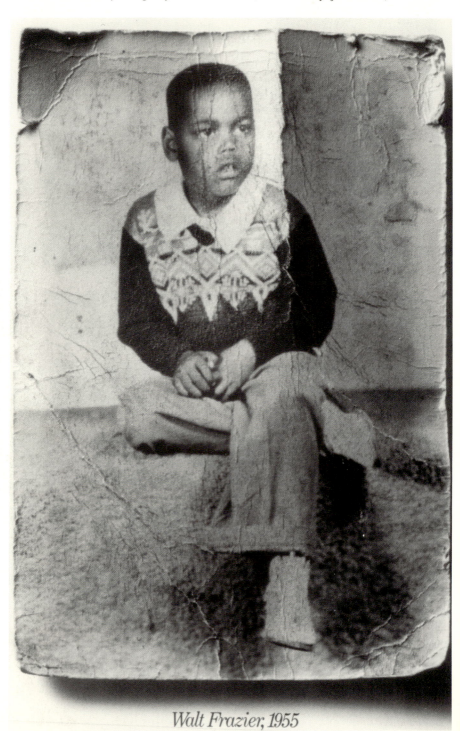

Walt Frazier, 1955

My sister Mary was eight and I was ten when we met Santa. After her came six more sisters and a total of fourteen years before I got myself a brother. (Photo courtesy of the author)

This is from my 1963 high school yearbook. Hazel Jackson was voted Howard High's most popular girl. Since I was the star of the basketball, football, and baseball teams, I was voted most athletic. (Photo courtesy of the author)

In the classroom at Southern Illinois University, I started to realize what an inferior education I had received up until then. I was scared at first, but got by with a little help from my friends. (Southern Illinois University Athletic Department)

At SIU, I was more at ease on the basketball court than in the classroom. But since we were a "small college," I still had doubts about my ability. (Southern Illinois University Athletic Department)

My first contract with the Knicks was for three years. Here I am at the formal signing with (from left to right) Knick coach Dick McGuire, my attorney Jim Zimmerman, and Knick general manager Eddie Donovan. Halfway through my rookie season, I didn't think I would last that long. (Southern Illinois University Athletic Department)

When I first came into the NBA, I was frequently scared and unsure on offense. But I felt I could defend against anyone, and that's how I was used—as a defensive stopper. Here I'm going against Paul Westphal. (Photo by George Kalinsky)

Before the Knicks traded for Dave DeBusschere—and I became a starter— I rarely drove to the hoop. (Photo by George Kalinsky)

After the trade, everything snapped into place and I began penetrating and shooting the jumper like I had in college. (Ken Regan/Camera 5)

As I became more comfortable on the court, I became more "Clyde," the well-dressed man-about-town. Clothes became my vice, and my tailor always had a suit for me on the mannequin. My Rolls also added to the Clyde image. I still have it today, but most of the time it stays in the garage. (Photos by George Kalinsky)

Making crucial free throws was one way I earned a reputation as a cool player. When the game and I were on the line, I rarely missed. (Ken Regan/Camera 5)

The starting five (left to right): Dick Barnett, me, Bill Bradley, Dave DeBusschere, and Willis Reed, after a playoff win. We weren't the tallest, fastest, or best jumpers. We were just the most intelligent team I've ever seen. (Photo courtesy of Basketball Hall of Fame)

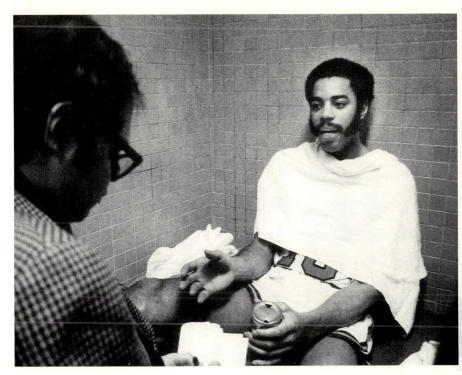

As I got more comfortable in New York, I found I liked talking to reporters and giving them good quotes. Sometimes the words in the newspapers were different from what I had said, but I still got a kick out of seeing my name in print. (Photo by George Kalinsky)

No one who played in the NBA ever had a bigger heart than Willis Reed. He gave you all he had, all the time, and not only demanded your respect, but earned it, too. (Photo by George Kalinsky)

Dave DeBusschere: Nobody intimidated The Butcher. (Ken Regan/Camera 5)

Nate Bowman (left, with Kareem Abdul Jabbar): He was more comfortable off the court. (Photo by George Kalinsky)

Dick Barnett: the old man. (Ken Regan/Camera 5)

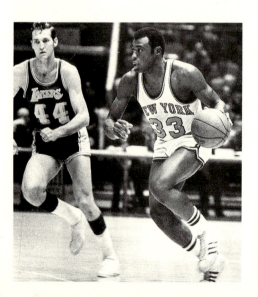

Mike Riordan: the captain of the subs. (Ken Regan/Camera 5)

Below left: *Cazzie Russell (right, with Jerry West): the shooter. (Photo by George Kalinsky)*

Below: *Dave Stallworth (right, with Jerry Lucas): The potential was unlimited. (Photo by George Kalinsky)*

No matter what happened, Red Holzman was always calm, always in control. And most important, he was always fair. (Ken Regan/Camera 5)

When we played Baltimore in the playoffs, it was the classic match-up: Clyde against Earl "The Pearl" Monroe. It was hand-to-hand combat, but even so, we became friends, out of mutual respect. (Photo by George Kalinsky)

Opposite, top left: *In the L.A. championship series, I had to guard Jerry West. Even today, I can still see that textbook jumper. (Ken Regan/Camera 5)*

Opposite, top right: *It might have taken Wilt Chamberlain a long time to get up in the air when we played the Lakers for the title, but once he did, he could still block shots and win games. (Note my superstitious shoelaces.) (Ken Regan/Camera 5)*

Opposite, bottom: *When we flew out to L.A. during the final series, we were pretty relaxed — as you can see. (Photo by George Kalinsky)*

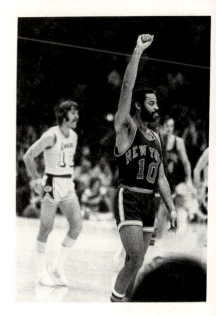

I tried never to show emotion on the court, but there were times — like when we won championships — when I couldn't help it. (Photo by George Kalinsky)

Willis was the first of the 1970 team to get his number retired by the Knicks; I was the second. Only Barnett's number hasn't been retired — and it should be. (Photo by George Kalinsky)

It was Red Holzman, the best coach I ever had, who presented me with my plaque when I was inducted into the Hall of Fame in 1987. If not for Red, I would never have made it there. (Photo courtesy of the author)

The Hall of Fame induction was a great occasion for me—the ultimate for a ballplayer. My son, Walt III, was there, along with my teammates Earl Monroe (left) and Phil Jackson. (Photo courtesy of the author)

I have a captain's license to pilot my boat—a thirty-eight-foot trimaran named Eula, after my mother—which I keep down in St. Croix. More than anything else today, sailing gives me the most pleasure. (Photo courtesy of the author)

to be careful who I was having drinks with. He didn't say any specific names, and didn't mention any specific places, so I didn't really know who he was talking about. I guess some undesirable—at least to management—people had been buying me drinks, but since I only hung out at high-class places, if there were undesirables around, what could I do about it? I assumed the warning wasn't that serious, just a reminder to be as careful as possible.

At all the places I hit during the night, I'd get half a drink at one of them and another half somewhere else. I was a sophomore in college before I ever drank a beer. The Butcher probably drank more at the end of one game than I did in a year. But when I got to the Knicks, I naturally wanted to be hip, so I started to drink rum and coke. Only problem was, it used to give me a terrible headache. When the hotel's wake-up call came at eight in the morning, I felt like somebody had taken a hammer to my brain.

There were no more drinks until I discovered wine. Wine made me talkative and sociable, and I could drink it without getting headaches. But two or three glasses were my limit. When I was already at the limit and fans wanted to buy me drinks, at first I'd tell them, "No thanks, I'm fine." Then a friend told me I shouldn't do that. "People will think you're saying you're too good for them, that you won't let them buy you a drink," he said. So I started accepting the offers, but leaving the glasses on the table. I'd sip slow and drink a bit of this glass and then somebody would buy me another and I'd have another sip or two. When I got up to leave, there'd be twelve or thirteen drinks sitting there on the bar, and I had never paid for any of them.

Free drinks weren't the only thing I found in the clubs. I found women, too. All kinds of women: pretty ones, ugly ones, fat ones, thin ones, old ones, young ones, they would all come on to me in the clubs and bars. When you're winning, you have a large selection of nice chicks. Since it became known that I used to hang out at Harry M.'s, women used to come there specifically to meet me. I'd sit at the bar, and each night seven or eight attractive women, top models and actresses, would come over. Cal Ramsey, who used to play for the Knicks and then was broadcasting the games, might walk over with a really terrific-looking woman. "Hey, Clyde," he'd say, "this lady told me she'd like to meet you."

I had always been shy with women. My sisters would have all their girlfriends over at the house, but I was so shy, I kept away from them, even though a lot of them liked me. In my school years, I didn't have many girlfriends and seldom went out. It was always difficult for me—and sometimes, still is— to just go over and start a conversation with someone. I might be able to finish things off, but breaking the ice was a problem. At school dances, I was the wallflower. I was scared of dancing because at home, when I tried, my sisters thought

I looked funny and laughed at me. I could dance slow a bit, but there were never enough slow songs. In college, I was a married man, and I took that seriously.

Only when I reached New York did I start to catch up on what I thought I had been missing. I was still shy, but in New York I didn't have to start things off. There was always someone coming over to me to say hello, and then I was able to go from there. Around the league, there were always women hanging around the arenas, waiting for you. The first year or two, I took them on. They were interchangeable, never far from the locker rooms, going to the same parties. The guys on the team shared them. A girl would leave one guy she was going with and go out with the next guy on the team and then the next. It slowly started to hit me that this was wrong. With all the women in the world, why should I have to go with someone who's just been with my teammate? I wondered about the players who would go with each other's girls, or try to. I started to lose respect for guys who would try to take away your girlfriend. I started thinking differently about the women who were always around. You gotta start looking for quality rather than quantity, I decided.

In New York, though, I found both. It was an ego trip, being young and famous and in New York. I never kept a phone number. Almost every chick I met would look better than the one I had before, so why did I need a phone book? If I met a woman tonight, I might not ever see her again, and I might not want to.

I liked women, but I didn't really love them. Unlike a lot of the guys, I could not have women around me constantly. Maybe I grew up with too many sisters. I needed my privacy, and after a couple of days with one woman around me, I would get bored and irritable. I'd see that it wouldn't work to stay together.

Sex was another matter. Whenever it was convenient, I had sex. That meant mostly after we played a game, not the nights before we played. I partied most every night, but if there was a game the next day, I gave myself a curfew and made sure I was back by midnight. My nights for women were mostly Tuesdays and Saturdays. The guys on the team would use the word "chosen" about getting together with a woman, like in "Hey, man, I heard you were chosen tonight." I was chosen often.

If I partied a lot in New York, on the road I usually rested. If I couldn't get it in the Big Apple, I felt, I couldn't find it anywhere. I agreed with what a New York cabbie once told me: "In New York, you either act crazy or go crazy."

I felt, too, that partying was good for me. It got me out of my room. I had only a couple of good friends, and my only constant companion was the television. I could not go to sleep without the television. If I came in at four in the morning, I'd turn the set on—I had to have it on—before I could fall asleep. If someone was there with me and turned it off, instinctively I'd wake up.

It took the trade to Cleveland, and leaving New York, to change me. I started to settle down when I went there. No more going out every night. In Cleveland, there weren't enough places to go. I could only be dangerous, I realized, in a dangerous environment.

In the second week of December, we beat the Bucks at Milwaukee again when Bradley came off a double pick down low and hit a jump shot from the left corner with twelve seconds to go. The play was designed for him, and Bill took the shot, but it could almost have been any of the guys. On other teams, when it came down to crunch time, there was usually one player they looked for. When we played Baltimore, we knew we had to stop Earl Monroe down the stretch. With the Lakers, Jerry West. There was usually only one player who wanted the ball when the pressure was on. Most guys didn't want it. You'd see them not making their cuts, moving away from the ball, letting their man stick close to them instead of trying to shake him.

On the Knicks, we all wanted it. If Willis or Barnett or I had been one-for-the-night, we still wanted the ball when the game was on the line. We figured the odds were with us. This sucker gotta go in this time. There were some games when

Bill or Dave didn't want it, when they hadn't been shooting well, or for some reason, just weren't feeling it. But when they were hot, they wanted it, and because Bill could shoot so quickly, we used to run a lot of plays for him at the end of games. Like Cazzie—but not in the same way—Bill knew how to get open for a shot and how to get it off. Cazzie would do it just by going up so quickly and always being ready to shoot. Bill did it by running and running and running, running his man around and around in circles until the guy was just too tired or too bored. Then, finally, Bill would be open and the shot would be there.

I'll never forget the first night Bradley played with the Knicks. He had been out of basketball for two years, after going off to study in England. After I had taken my $25,000 over the summer, Bill had just signed a mid-season contract for around $500,000 for four years to come back, play for the Knicks, and, everybody said, save the franchise. He was the white hope, and the Knicks had held a huge press conference to announce his signing.

He played his first game in December 1967, at the Garden. There were so many reporters and others in the locker room to talk to Bill and to report on the smallest details about him, even down to the way he dressed for the game, that the players were almost forced out of our own locker room to get dressed.

During the warm-up, when Bradley touched the ball, the

fans cheered. He made a lay-up, and they cheered some more. When he bent down to tie his shoe, they cheered. I had never seen a crowd react that way before.

I was curious to see him play, too. He played pretty well that night, but then, near the end of the game, he blew it for the Knicks by throwing up a bad shot. The crowd booed him. Welcome to New York, Bill.

Still, I was impressed. I thought, Wow, the guy is terrific, particularly for not having played much for a couple of years. I was most impressed with his passing. He made some great blind passes, really threading the ball. It was obvious he was a ballplayer, even if he didn't really look like one.

He didn't have a ballplayer's body, with his big butt and his shoulders sloped all the way down. He couldn't run very fast and was not an exceptional jumper. But in practice, he'd shoot fifty to one hundred shots from the same spot. He wanted perfection, and he had the discipline to continue shooting until he thought he had it. The whole team would be finished practicing, and Bill would still be out there, working on his shot. If I'd shoot twenty-five free throws in a row, I'd feel I was doing good. That'd be enough. I couldn't shoot anymore because I was too tired and it was too boring. Bill could shoot two hundred free throws in a row.

He understood the game and knew how to compensate for what he didn't have. On defense, Bill didn't have good lateral movement, but he worked at it. He always got good position, which he knew he had to do. He was an intelligent player. It didn't help him much in the beginning, though. With his big contract and publicity, the whole NBA was gunning for him, looking to show him up. He was a guard then, and as soon as he got into the game, the other team would start running clear-outs. Here's Bradley and let's get the ball to Oscar, or to Hal Greer or Lenny Wilkens, and let's see what the Princeton man can do.

The answer was, not much. Standing out there on the court it was easy to catch a cold, with every player just rushing by Bradley. "The chump," Barnett said. "He couldn't guard a man in a phone booth." Only after he switched to forward did Bradley stop hurting us defensively. As a forward, he was able to make up for his lack of quickness and use his smarts.

He may have had the publicity and the big contract, but Bill never showed it off. Cazzie, who had had the same kind of monster deal, always flaunted it. He'd walk around in the hotel or at the airport with *The Wall Street Journal* tucked under his arm, just to make sure you could see it. Even if you didn't ask, he'd tell you about the stocks he owned and the new car he was buying. It was his way of saying, Hey, man, you see how much money I'm making? On the other hand, Dollar Bill probably looked like the poorest guy on the Knicks. Instead of a flashy car, like Cazzie's, he drove a beat-up old Volkswagen. He'd be on the team plane, take off his sports jacket, and you'd see he had a hole in his shirt. Clothes weren't important to him, and Barnett was always on his case about his wardrobe.

"Hey, Dollar, who's your tailor? Mr. Goodwill?"

"You pay somebody for those pants? You jivin' me, Dollar? Some mutha took real money for them?"

Bill wore a trenchcoat that the Salvation Army would've refused. At one time, I think it was beige, but it had become sort of a mix, a little brown, some green, gray, black, whatever had stuck to it. If it rained or was pretty cold, Bill would wear it, which was bad enough. When he didn't have it on, he would ball it up and carry it under his arm. It was getting embarrassing. Here we were, the New York Knicks, leading the league, on the covers of the magazines, and with a sophisticated, well-dressed reputation to uphold. I think the original idea was Willis's. When Bill was out on the court one practice day working on his free throws, we stole the trenchcoat. Everybody, including Red, chipped in, and we bought Bradley a new one, clean and fashionable. "Bill," we told him, "your coat's disgusting. This new one, you gotta wear it. And you gotta take good care of it and keep it in good shape."

It took time for Bradley to fit in with the team, not just as a player, but also as an individual. He was always a pretty quiet guy, and at the beginning, I got the feeling he couldn't relax with us. He was different, and he knew it. With his money, his background, and his education, he knew he wasn't one of the boys. He was an Ivy Leaguer, and back then the NBA wasn't always a first-class organization. As Barnett used to say about him, "Bradley's as straight up as twelve o'clock." Particularly with the black players, he seemed to be on the outside looking in. When the blacks would toss street slang at him, I don't think he understood what they were saying. It was funny in a sense, because Bill was the least prejudiced player I've ever met. Gillette would come to him with all their grooming products offering him piles of money if he would endorse something and Bill always said no. But if I came up to him and said, "Hey, Bill, can you come up to Harlem and talk to some kids?" he always said sure. He'd go to Harlem regularly to talk to kids and give clinics, and never accepted a cent for any of the trips.

In his first couple of years, some of the white players, like Phil Jackson, Dick Van Arsdale, and Mike Riordan, tried to communicate with him and get him to relax and open up. But it was DeBusschere coming to New York that finally brought Bradley out. Dave and Bill really liked each other, and Dave, who was loose and comfortable in the locker room, mellowed Bill. Bill started having a beer with Dave now and then, and he started learning to relax and not to take everything so seriously. Little by little, he did become one of the boys, and the game became fun for him.

I wasn't on the court when Bill made the jumper to give us the win. With a few minutes gone in the fourth quarter, while I was running up the court, I slipped on a spot of wet floor. I got up and tried to run, but I felt as if I were doing it in slow motion. There was a dull ache way down in my crotch, not a severe pain, but when I pushed my legs to move faster, they didn't react. At the next time-out, I told Red, "I can't run, man. I gotta sit."

During the NBA season, you get used to playing hurt. You have to. Everybody has something nagging him. Right now, Willis had a bad toe, some of the other guys had bruises here and there. The body just wears down, and you have to cope with it. A few players even play better when they're hurt. It's like you're a wounded animal, more alert to what's going on. You understand that when you're hurt, you have to work harder, you have to compensate mentally and by hustling for what the body doesn't do as well.

"It's a groin pull," Danny tells me. That means that no matter how hard I try, there's not much I can do about it. Groin pulls aren't terrible. They just don't go away very easily, and there's always a risk of them getting worse. You try not to overextend it, but you never know when you're going to stretch your leg too wide and pull it more. I'll give it some heat and I'll give it some ice, and still the only way for it to really heal is with rest. I probably could have played with the pull, but with the team's record at 27–3, Red had a little room to maneuver. He let me sit out the next game, which was a good thing. I needed the rest. The morning of the next game, I woke up and felt like Dracula had drained all the blood from my body. I was exhausted. I couldn't move. Maybe it was psychological, and I was using the groin pull as an out. I knew I didn't have to play, and maybe my body knew it, too.

With me not playing, we lost to Seattle, and then to Philly and Atlanta after I came back. That made it four losses out of the last five games, our worst stretch of the season. For the month after the winning streak ended, we were just a little bit better than a .500 ballclub. And when you start to lose, you begin to feel even more tired. During the streak, it seemed we all had so much energy, night after night, game after game. A few losses and you start hearing about fatigue and about injuries, about ankles that are sore and my toe hurts and this guy doesn't give me the ball enough.

We were out in Chicago playing the Bulls and some of the little aggravations came to a head. We were leading the game, but not playing real well. During a time-out, Red got on my case.

"Clyde, you're some damn all-star," he screamed at me. "What the hell are you doin' out there? You in the game or what? Block your fuckin' man and get him off the boards."

What the hell is he screaming at me for? I wondered. I'm not the only one out there screwing up. And we got the damn game anyway, and there's not much time left. Why the hell is he angry with me? "What do you want from me,

Red?" I screamed back at him. "I'm not doing any worse than anybody else. And hey, man, the damm game is over anyway."

"I'll tell you when the fuckin' game is over. You're not the coach. I am."

I tried to say something else, and Red told me to shut up. "I get the last word," he shouted, "and the first word, and all the rest of the words in between."

There was nothing else I could say. I went back into the game, and I hated Red. I could've killed the man. I ran up and down the court for a few minutes, got my body hot again, and somehow the anger evaporated. We won the game, and I forgot about the argument. Red forgot, too. No one mentioned the screaming and the shouting. One of the best things about Red is that he doesn't hold grudges. Neither do I.

On Christmas night at the Garden, we were down by one to the Pistons with about fifteen seconds to go. Dollar made another double-pick jumper to put us up by one, but then Detroit came right down, Bellamy drove around Willis to score, and we were down by one. As Bells's shot fell through, we called a time-out. There was one second showing on the clock as we huddled around Red. "There's not much we can do," he said, "except try the play." There was only one play he could mean.

It's another play we borrowed from Boston, which used to run it for Bill Russell. We practiced it over and over again in practice, and it never worked. Not once. Never. I threw the ball up from far away and Willis was supposed to dunk it, without ever bringing the ball down. That was the idea. In practice, I'd throw the ball over the backboard, I'd throw it short, I'd throw it everywhere but right by the hoop. It became one of the team's favorite jokes, with everybody laughing at me as they saw me trying time after time to get the ball to Willis. "Hey, Clyde," Red would call out, "let's just try to get it close this time, okay?"

This time we had no choice. Because of the time-out, we got the ball at half court. Everybody lined up on the free-throw line, with Barnett on the extreme right end and Willis in the middle. The ref handed me the ball. Rich picked Bellamy, and Willis rolled around toward the basket. I threw a perfect lob pass and the ball just hung at the rim. Willis went up and guided the ball gently in just as time ran out. The Pistons stood there, all of them with their mouths wide open. We ran off the court laughing, just like we had stolen the apple from the teacher's desk.

After we finished laughing, showered, and got dressed, we left for the killer road trip of the season: seven thousand miles in ninety-six hours, to play four games. Thursday night in New York to Friday night in L.A. to Saturday night against Seattle in Vancouver to Sunday night in Phoenix back on Monday night against Chicago in New York. Fasten your seat belts.

I've never liked flying very much, but I've grown used to it. Going out west usually wasn't too bad, because the skies were generally clear and there wasn't too much bouncing around. We flew first class, because that's part of the players' contract. We need the room. Think of being 6′ 4″ or 6′ 8″ in a coach seat. If the flight is longer than an hour, it has to be first class. If it's a trip just up to Boston, they can stick us anywhere, and it's tight, and really uncomfortable for the big guys. In first class, we can spread out and relax.

For the first couple of hours, I sat by Barnett, listening to his stories about the old days back at Tennessee State and in the American Basketball League, which hadn't lasted very long. When Barnett got ready to begin his steady card game with Cazzie and Bowman, I moved over to Danny Whalen, to listen a little to his stories about his old days as a baseball trainer. With a few hours still to go, I wandered back to my own seat and put on my tape recorder to listen to some Marvin Gaye and Smokey Robinson. The tape recorder, which was a big and heavy old-fashioned reel-to-reel machine, was my road partner. It killed me to lug it across the country, but it was my only companion. Bowman had a nice little portable cassette machine that sounded real nice, but he'd always play jazz on it, and I hated jazz. My machine might have been heavy, but at least I had *my* music.

A couple of rows ahead, Bradley had his head buried in a book. Mike Riordan had about four or five newspapers spread out in front of him. Willis was looking at some financial reports for a restaurant he owned. The plane was pretty quiet. With Smokey Robinson in my ears, I fastened my seat belt and drifted off to sleep. While traveling, I can sleep like a dead man, snap my fingers and I'm off. If you're a pro basketball player, it's a good skill to have. When we land, I think we're just taking off.

The hours and the days went by in a blur. Our movements were conditioned responses. It was Christmastime, but out west there were·very few decorations. And though it should've been cold for the holidays, it was warm. This is awful, I thought. I'm glad I never grew up out here.

We walked into the hotel in L.A., and a middle-aged man comes over to us. "Hey, you guys the Globetrotters?" he asked none of us in particular.

"No, man, we're jockeys," Willis answered him. "We're in town for a jockeys' convention."

We had the Lakers down by almost 20 in the third quarter, and I loved hearing how quiet the crowd was. They had been booing us and cheering the Lakers, and we had shut them up. But in the fourth quarter, West did it again to us and the crowd got loud and we lost it.

I lay in bed in the hotel in Vancouver, watching TV, and a voice came on and said, "This is KXOL in San Francisco," and I said to myself, wait a minute. Where am I? Is this San Francisco or Vancouver or . . . where is it exactly?

After beating the Sonics, while we were in the locker room DeBusschere whispered to me, "Walt, get his shoestrings." Dollar was talking to someone and didn't see me when I pulled the laces out of his shoes. Later on, at the airport, he clomped down the aisles with his shoes flapping all over the place. Bill didn't say anything about it, as though maybe he hadn't noticed, but he was smiling, a little.

In the coffee shop at the hotel in Phoenix, a waitress asked Willis if he was Wilt Chamberlain. I think Wilt's the only player people out there had ever heard of. Willis told her, "Sure I am, ma'am," and then signed an autograph with Wilt's name.

Considering how tight the trip was, it was incredible there were no airline screw-ups. On another trip a month later, our bags, including all the uniforms, went on one plane, while the team went on another, because of fog at the airport. The bags didn't arrive until just before game time.

Walking through the airport, waiting for the bus, standing in the hotel lobby, we were always stared at by people. "They must be basketball players," we could hear them saying. Maybe they'd never seen tall people before. Some of the guys might have been uncomfortable with it, but I liked them staring at us. It was one of the reasons I made sure to dress nicely when traveling, because I knew we would get the looks. Red didn't have any dress code for the team. We didn't have to wear ties and jackets all the time. He just wanted us to be neat, like my mother did. Phil Jackson, when he traveled with us, always wore jeans. Neat ones. I don't think Phil even owned a tie.

After beating the Suns in Phoenix, we got right back on a plane and flew across the country. We arrived back in New York at 5:00 A.M., before the sun was up. I shared a cab back to the New Yorker with the Rave, Bowman, and Barnett. As soon as we got in the taxi, Nate put his big foot up by the driver's face. The driver ignored it and headed into the sunrise and Manhattan. "Hey, man," Bowman started in on him. "Why you takin' the tunnel? Why didn't you take the Fifty-ninth Street Bridge?" The driver was in a no-win situation. If he had taken the bridge, the guys would have gotten on him and said, "Why the hell didn't you take the tunnel?" The guys were hoping to upset him, so he'd get angry and then we wouldn't have to tip him when we got to the hotel. For the whole trip, they stayed on his case. "Hey, man, you're going too fast." "Hey, why you stoppin' at that light for?" "This ain't the right lane to be in." When we got to the hotel, the cabbie was so pissed, he didn't care about the tip, or even the fare itself. Another victory for the player's wallet.

I had about three or four hours of sleep on the flight back, and I was still tired, but when I got to my room, I couldn't get into bed right away. Phil Jackson, one of my first Knick roomies, told me that when he was tired and couldn't sleep, he wouldn't try to force it. He'd try to do something, go for a walk, have a good time. The worst thing to do, he told me, was try to go to sleep and then you can't. Then you're more tired than ever. I read the newspaper a little, watched some late-night TV, and finally got to sleep around ten or eleven in the morning. By the middle of the afternoon, I was up.

That night against the Bulls, I saw very early that I wasn't sharp. My reflexes, my agility, my timing were off, and I wasn't the only one. We played like we were tired, which made sense. My jumper hit the front rim a lot, and sometimes the back rim, and sometimes no rim at all. But the biggest problem when you're tired is getting back on defense. We were all moving slowly, sluggishly, getting back a step or two later than usual, and not picking up our own men. Still, the crowd at the Garden, as always, was cheering us, and that psyched us. When you're fatigued, you need something to give you that extra spark and push you past what your body tells you it can do. With the crowd behind us, we did things methodically, but we were doing them. This is, I think, what it means to be a professional: to go out and play a credible game when you're not feeling it. We beat the Bulls by 20.

The day after we returned from the road was the last day of 1969. To celebrate New Year's Eve, some of us were invited to a big party hosted by Knick fan Woody Allen, at a large apartment over on the East Side. Woody greeted us wearing a fancy tuxedo, instead of his usual plaid shirt and jeans. I was surprised; then I looked down and saw that he had sneakers on.

I guess it made sense that entertainers like to hang around with pro ballplayers. In a sense, we were entertainers, too. We had ham in us. Some guys say they'd rather play ball with nobody in the stands at all. Not me. The cheers and the screaming juiced me. The awareness that thousands of people were watching every move I made pushed me, made me want to play the best I possibly could. When we played in our first nationally televised game of the year, I thought of it as a showcase. Back then, the NBA wasn't on TV nearly as much as it is now. There was no cable or super stations or ESPN, and only one game a week would be seen throughout the country. This was one of the few times before the play-offs when you could really make yourself a reputation. If I played well on national TV, it would be remembered for a long time.

In the first half of the televised game, I dribbled behind my back a few times and put on a few other showtime moves. I thought, still, that I did everything in the flow of the game. Afterward, a newspaper reported that some of my team-mates had criticized me for holding on to the ball too much and showing off for the tube too much. No specific names were mentioned, and no one said anything to me about it. I assumed it wasn't anyone, just the press again. Usually when any of us had something to say, a gripe or a problem, we'd call a team meeting to get it off our chests. When there were rumors about problems flying around, or we read quotes like that in the papers, Willis would say, Let's meet, so we could air it out. He didn't call one this time. Once again, I figured, the reporters had their own ideas.

To celebrate the new year, Red had us practice on the first day of January out at St. John's University in Queens. Because the Garden was also the home for the New York Rangers hockey team, the Ice Capades, the circus, and I don't know what else, it was always booked up on our off-days. We had to practice all over the city, at armories, community colleges, a school for the deaf, and at something called the Lost Battalion Hall. Today, the Knicks have a long-term deal with a state university campus for a fancy training camp and practice facility that gives them three courts, a weight room, a trainer's room, coaches' offices, a video center, and locker room. We would've been happy just to know we were going to the same place every time.

Nobody liked practice, but you only really hate it when you're losing. When the team is winning most of the time, practice can be fun.

Our practices were always pretty basic. They'd last around two hours, including about forty-five minutes of actual running. The rest of the time we spent walking through the plays, going over Barry and the cross and 22 for the ten-thousandth time during the season. We'd go over the same defenses, blue for the full-court press and red for the man-to-man pressure all over the floor, and the half-court red. There was always a lot of talking and trying to figure out how we could make the plays work more efficiently than they had been.

Nate and Willis pushed each other pretty hard during the practice, and the Rave and DeBusschere also had a few hard shoves between them. Red would break everything up before anything got out of hand. I thought that he was pleased, though. It was good that the guys were still hungry and not becoming complacent. The players who weren't starting were continuing to push, wanting to take the places of the starters. Everybody was playing hard, even in practice.

Nobody played harder than Mike Riordan. Mike didn't run for the forty-five minutes—he ran for the entire two hours. He never stopped moving. Even on the road, where in theory he had a lot of free time and could relax a little, he was always standing up and reading a folded newspaper while he'd eat a sandwich. I never saw Mike sit down to eat a meal.

Hustling was how Mike had become a pro ballplayer. Realistically, he shouldn't have been in the NBA. When he first came to the Knicks, he couldn't shoot and he couldn't handle the ball very well. He was probably the player with the least amount of natural talent who ever made it in the league. But Mike could run, and he was strong. When we guarded each other in practice, he'd just as soon run over me than around me. His first season with the Knicks, his job was to intentionally commit a foul, to give one when it made sense strategically. Mike didn't just give a foul, though. He smashed a foul. He'd knock the hell out of a guy. Mike worked as hard as anybody, and developed a pretty good outside shot and a terrific drive where he'd just blow by his man like a rocket. He became the captain of the bench, the number-one backcourt sub. Mike never had an injury. He came to practice with his shoes, his socks, and his jock, and that was all. When all the other guys and I were busy taping this and taping that, fixing ankles and knees and calves, Mike just got dressed and went out to play. He never taped anything, not even his ankles, and he never got hurt.

Near the end of January, the season stopped for a few days. I would have liked a rest and I could have used one. But while the rest of the team flew home after a loss in Boston, Willis, DeBusschere, and I went on to Philadelphia for the all-star game. I was on the team for the first time, a starter for the East Squad. Oscar Robertson and I were in the backcourt, with Willis, Gus Johnson, and Billy Cunningham up front. I was in awe.

I sat in the locker room at the Philadelphia Spectrum

and I don't think I said a word during all the time getting ready before we went out on the floor. It was just an honor to be in the same locker room with these guys, listening to them, watching them. I just wanted to observe. These guys were my idols. What made them tick? Was there something all of them had in common?

Oscar was quiet, very laid-back, reserved, and straight up. He's almost a square, you know? I thought.

Gus was smoking, and very talkative, moving around the locker room and joking with everybody. Billy Cunningham was hyper, couldn't sit still, jumping around, acting just the way he plays. I had liked the way he played, both when he was at college at North Carolina and with the Sixers. He was a white player who could really jump, one of the few, and he was a tough competitor, never giving an inch. Around that time, I got an offer to do an endorsement for a kids' toy. The company told me they also needed a white player, a star, and I thought of Billy and told them to try to get Cunningham to do the commercial with me. They did, and he was an easy guy to get along with.

I didn't care if I played much in the game. I wouldn't have minded sitting on the bench watching all these guys play. When I was a kid, these were the basketball names—the only names—I had heard. Oscar. Elgin. Wilt. We never needed last names. If you didn't know who they were, man, you just weren't paying attention.

With all the superstars in the game, at first no one wanted to take charge. It wasn't the way it is in today's all-star games, where everybody wants to slam and jam it and put on his own private showtime. Then, no one wanted to show anyone else up. These were great ballplayers, but they were unselfish ballplayers, too. Even in an all-star game, they always had the team in mind. Everybody wanted the same thing, just to play well together. Players were passing up moves they'd normally make as they tried to fit into the team scheme of things, and so there were a lot of turnovers early in the game. For the first quarter, particularly, everybody was throwing the ball away and we were just plain out of sync. Me, too. I was playing with guys I'd idolized, and I didn't want to do anything to disrupt the flow of the game. I just wanted to fit in, and show I belonged.

Slowly, the players realized, hey, this isn't working, and they started to become more comfortable going for their moves. They started trying to get their points, and the flow of the game became better. Near the end of the third quarter and in the last period, we played the way we normally played: moving the ball around, trying to get the good shot. That's the way to win, and we did. I was glad, but I wouldn't have been too upset if we had lost. The all-star game is fun. It's supposed to be. Well, at least it was fun the first few years I played in it. But then, after several seasons of my being named to the team, all my friends started saying, Hey, man, when're you gonna do something at the all-star game? When're you gonna win the MVP? The game, like all the other ones, became pressure and less fun, because I started thinking, Yeah, I would like to be MVP one time in the game. Finally, in 1975, I was named the all-star Most Valuable Player. My friends stopped asking about it and left me alone.

It's been almost twenty years since my first all-star game, and I realize today that I was on the court then with most of the players who would be on my all-time all-star team. The best players I ever saw. The best players I can ever imagine. Oscar Robertson and Jerry West, Wilt Chamberlain, Bill Russell, Elgin Baylor, and Kareem Abdul-Jabbar. Yeah, it's a six-man team, but I had to add Kareem because of what he's done and how long he's done it. How can I leave him off?

These were all players who could dominate the game from their positions, whatever positions they played. At any point, these six could simply take the game over, and change its direction. They could all do so many different things. Elgin could bring the ball up and get the ball off the backboards. Wilt could score and could pass it off. West played defense, and like Kareem, he could have scored a lot more points if he'd been selfish. All of them made the guys they played with better. With the exception of Russell, they were all unstoppable offensive players. Once they got on a roll, good-bye. And Russell was the most dominant defensive player who ever lived. Russell was so good, he was scary. And when you didn't see him, that was when you were scared the most. You didn't know where he was, and he could be lurking around anywhere. Then you'd go up for your shot and, suddenly, he'd be there, and the ball was rolling down the court in the other direction. Whenever we had a fast break against Russell, I made sure to be the trailer, figuring I could pick up the ball after he had blocked the first man down.

These guys were supermen, and they would have been the best no matter when they played. They not only had incredible natural talent, they worked at it, too, always improving. Right behind the top six, just a silly millimeter behind, I'd put Larry Bird and Doctor J, John Havlicek and maybe Magic Johnson, and me. Willis would be there, too, if all his injuries hadn't held him back. These were terrific players, but still not as good as the best.

By the second week of February, we were leading the second-place Bucks by half a dozen games in the standings, before playing the Celtics at the Garden. I woke up that morning about my usual time, with my head swimming. I felt dizzy and weak all over. I got up from my bed and almost fell down. It was the flu, or a cold, or something, and I knew there was no way that I could play that night. I thought immediately of calling Red and telling him that, but I knew there was no way that he'd accept it. He never had. It had happened before. You'd call Red and he'd tell you, "Come over here anyway. See the doctor. If you're really sick, you'd have to see the doc anyway." It was like having to get a note from your teacher. The best thing to do was just get out of the hotel, drag my sick body across the street, and show the man, hey, I really was sick. I did it, saw the doctor, which I would've had to do anyway, convinced everybody that I was dying, and finally dragged myself back to the room to get some rest.

I wasn't the only Knick to miss the game. A few days before, Bradley had torn a ligament in his ankle. At first no one thought it was serious, and he tried to go, but now he couldn't play, either. My flu went away and I came back for the next game, but Dollar was out for more than a month, sixteen games in a row. Cazzie, who had lost his position as a starter to Bill when *he* broke his ankle the season before, stepped right back into the starting lineup. At first it didn't look like we had lost anything. Two nights later, at Philadelphia, we ripped them apart with 80 points in the first half and a 151–106 win, the worst defeat ever for the Philadelphia franchise. It felt like practice, and we could do anything we wanted. The Knicks once again looked like the machine they had been. Maybe even better.

But the Knicks were a funny team. We were a club that never outrebounded anybody, and really didn't outshoot many teams, either. We weren't the fastest or the best jumpers. We didn't have any guys who could physically dominate the other teams, wipe them out with just God-given talent. What made the Knicks unique was that the parts fit together, like hands in a glove. When we played together, the Knicks won because we were the most intelligent team. No team could outthink us, and no team outhustled us. We knew how to win. When the game was on the line, we *were* the best shooters and played the best defense and ran a fast break as well as anyone. I've seen pro basketball for twenty years now, and I've never seen a team as intelligent as those Knicks. Maybe the Russell-Havlicek-K.C. Jones Celtics were close. But our intelligence made us unique.

Chemistry is accidental. There's no way of planning it and no way of knowing how to put it back together when it's not there anymore. When the chemistry is right, you take it for granted. And when it's not there, you can't remember exactly how you did it, what way things worked, how we did it so good. Management had brought in good players, but that didn't mean we'd all play well together. What helped was that with the exception of Barnett, we all had similar backgrounds as players. We had been brought up to believe in a team system, both offensively and defensively. We'd had coaches who had stressed the fundamentals. We weren't self-ish. We weren't all friends, but we had respect for each other. Dave and Bill and Willis were friendly, and Dick was tight with Nate and the Rave and Cazzie. You don't have to be friends to play ball together. You don't even have to like the coach to play ball together for him. But you can't have guys playing together who don't respect one another and don't respect the coach.

Because we were such a delicately balanced team, when Dollar went out with his ankle injury, we lost more than just one starter. Cazzie had a terrific ability, and the team suffered from it. He was the type of player who scored a lot of points, more than Bill, but he didn't make the players around him better. Cazzie knew how to get his own shot. He'd look for it. When he got the ball, the ball didn't go any farther. It didn't move because Cazzie, wherever he got it, could create on his own. He didn't need anybody's help. With him in there, we were four other guys standing around while Muscles Russell did his thing. And when Cazzie wasn't shooting well, like all good gunners he'd try to force his shots and take more and more of them, until they started to drop. A lot of the times, he'd shoot from his favorite spot in the corner, which put our defense out of kilter, and if he missed that made us vulnerable to the fast break. The other team would get the rebound and off they'd go, with us outnumbered at the other end.

Bradley made us all better because of the continuity he gave us. With his constant movement, he made us a cohesive unit. We all knew that Bill couldn't get his own shot, the way Cazzie could, so we had to get it for him. Red would say, "You gotta get Bradley involved in this. Move it around and get him a shot." Because Bill kept moving, the ball kept moving. We had very few plays for me, or for Willis, but we had to have a few for Bill. Bill wouldn't try to go one-on-one. He relied on us to set picks for him and get the ball to him when he was open. If he got the ball and didn't have the shot, he'd reverse it and we'd run another option off the play. His running set up the backdoor plays and the open outside shots for the rest of us.

For a month or so, we muddled along without Bill while it became obvious to all of us who should be the starter. There had been a lot of controversy for two seasons about it. Both Bill and Cazzie had come into the NBA with so much publicity and such big contracts, they were always set against each other. It was that way in the press, and it became a little that way in real life, too. Cazzie was always running Bill down, talking to Stallworth and Bowman, dealing in lots of petty stuff about how he should've been starting. He never mentioned any of it to me, or to Willis or Dave, because we never wanted to get involved in that kind of cheap chicanery. In practice, Bill and Cazzie would always be pushing and shoving, harder maybe than they needed to just for a practice. They were always trying to show Red—and maybe each other—who was better.

We won ten of sixteen with Cazzie starting. Dollar returned to the court on March 14, to help us beat the Rockets in San Diego and clinch the regular-season Eastern Division championship. It was the first time the Knicks had won anything since I had been with them, the first time the franchise had taken any kind of title in almost twenty years. "You haven't done anything yet," Red reminded us. "You haven't accomplished anything. This is just one leg of a long race."

Though we ran off the floor slapping some hands and some backs, there was no real excitement to the clinching, or much emotion to the celebration. Ever since November, we had expected to win the championship, and it was no big thing. We knew we could do it, it was just a matter of time. And we also knew that in the months since the streak had ended, we had played all right, but not the way we had before. We didn't even have the best record in the league over that period. Milwaukee did.

We had known for a long time we were going to win it and had actually expected to clinch the night before, in Portland. That was where the champagne was. But we had lost to the Trailblazers. Tonight there was no champagne. We had to move on right after the game to Los Angeles the next night and there was no real time for a celebration, and no TV cameras to record it and egg us on. We weren't an emotional team anyway, and everybody just got dressed in a hurry so we could catch our plane. "Hey, man," Barnett said, "this is the wildest party since V-J day in Tokyo."

Waiting at the San Diego airport, we got pizzas for everyone, our fancy celebration meal. Then we found out that our flight was canceled because our plane had a flat tire. The only other plane available to take us to L.A. didn't have a qualified pilot. We waited a long time to get our bags back, and then returned to the hotel for a few hours of sleep before we finally flew out to L.A. early the next morning.

Against the Lakers, I pulled the groin muscle again. I couldn't extend my leg and had to come out of the game. Maybe if we hadn't clinched and the play-offs weren't coming up, I could have played. I was able to go front and back, but not sideways. There was no lateral movement and I'd have had trouble guarding my man. On offense, I wouldn't be able to take that big first step, to explode to the basket. It wasn't terrible, but I was hurting. As the regular season ran down, I wasn't the only one. Willis sat out a few games so he could rest his knees, which had been hurting him for a long time, and which he strained a bit more when we played Atlanta a few weeks earlier. DeBusschere in general was all beat up. Bradley's ankle still wasn't perfect.

For life-and-death games, we all probably could have played. Life and death was coming up, so Red let us rest. Banged up and exhausted, with some of the guys on the bench, we ended the season by losing our last four games in a row, our longest losing streak of the year. The games weren't important, we all said. We were, we told ourselves, ready for the play-offs.

CHAPTER

7

FOR WINNING THE REGULAR SEASON EASTERN Division title and for having the best record in the league over eighty-two games, we won a few bucks. Twenty-five thousand dollars total, split up among the team. Peanuts, considering the effort we had put out. We had won sixty games already, and it didn't mean a thing. Now we had a twenty-one-game season, and all it meant was everything. If we didn't win now, our excellent year would go down the drain. I wished they'd already put the whole damn year in the record books.

In a way, I hated the play-offs. There wasn't very much money to be made in them, but our pride and prestige would be gone if we lost. We had more on the line than anybody. Ever since the eighteen-game winning streak, everybody—including us—expected the Knicks to win it all. The play-offs, though, were also where you gained your notoriety. If I wanted to be considered the best guard in the league, it would be because of what I did for the next month. Everybody would be watching us, and watching me.

Our first round opponents were the Baltimore Bullets, who we'd knocked out of the play-offs the season before, beating them four straight. Nine of the last ten times we'd played them, we'd come out on top, yet I still thought they'd probably be our toughest opponent throughout the play-offs. The year before, the Bullets had won the regular-season title in the East, and they probably had as much firepower as any club in the league. They also matched up very well against us. Oh yeah, it would be a series of classic matchups. Widebody Wes Unseld, who had been the league's Most Valuable Player a year ago, against Willis, this season's MVP. DeBusschere against Gus Johnson: the two best all-around forwards in the league, the hardest-working against the flashiest, the man who shattered backboards way before Darryl Dawkins started doing it. Bradley, the man in motion, against Jack Marin, the Bullets' Bradley, a great outside shooter who was always running and dodging behind screens.

And the Bullets had Earl Monroe. Clyde against the Pearl. The saying around the league was that even Jesus Christ himself couldn't go one-on-one with Earl. Earl was the greatest offensive player I've ever seen, better than Oscar, better than West. With Oscar, I knew what he wanted to try to do with me, use his brute strength and push me down lower and lower. With West, I knew he was first going to look for the outside jumper. He wasn't going to try any fancy moves. With Earl, I never knew what he was going to do. I don't think he did, either.

Earl was the hardest player in the league for me to defend. My defense was based on intelligence, on knowing what the opponent was going to do, on playing my man's tendencies. Earl didn't have any tendencies. Each time he brought the ball downcourt, he started with a new deck. I could try to push Oscar farther out and try to force West to his left, but when I forced Earl to his left, he would spin right. When I forced him right, he'd spin left.

Still, I liked going up against him. I liked the rivalry. Me against him, hand-to-hand combat. If we were going to win, I knew I had to contain Earl. If he got 40, and he could do that, we were not going to win it. The whole Bullet offense was geared around him, getting the ball out quickly to him and then getting him out on the break. With all the shots he got because of the way they played, I could do a good job on him and he could still get 35.

My reputation was on the line against him. With his showmanship game, it was embarrassing the things he did to guys. He'd have you moving left when he went up from the right, have you coming down when he was going up. If he burned me, everyone would know, because in the play-offs, everything gets magnified.

Life is more intense during the play-offs. There's no more time to pace yourself. Everybody goes all out all the time because there's no other way. Both offensively and defensively, the tempo is up. The crowds are roaring from the time the lineups are introduced until the last peanut seller has gone home.

The play-offs are all about execution. Everybody knows the plays you're going to run, what moves you have, and what liabilities you're trying to hide. During the regular season, it might be a couple of months from the time we played a team until we saw them again. Now we'd be playing the same guys game after game. During the season, you'd find out about other teams' weaknesses—now, in the play-offs, you'd try to work on them. We'd try to get Gus Johnson to shoot from the outside and lay off Unseld, who didn't look to score, to help out on the other Bullets. During the season, the Bullets hadn't tried very much to isolate Bradley, with his defensive liabilities, one-on-one. Now they would. They'd try to get me to follow my nose to the ball too much and have my man go backdoor on me. Both teams would look for any advantage they could find.

On March 26, the series opened at the Garden. Red finished his pregame talk, and you could tell that we were up. Barnett yelled over to the trainer's room, "Hey, Danny, what time does this fracas start, man?"

"Just a few minutes, Rich. You'll be there in time."

"Yeah, man," I said. "Let's get it on now."

Bradley, usually one of the quietest guys in the locker room, said, "Yeah, Clyde, come on. Let's go out there and do it."

There are no cheerleaders on this club, but everyone was standing now, and we all put our hands together in the center, with Willis putting his huge paw on top. "All *right,* let's *do* it," he said, and then he turned and led us out the door and onto the court. John Condon, the P.A. man, called out our names, and the roar started. It fires you up.

The Pearl was dealing from the opening tap. In the first couple of minutes, he hit a jump shot, made a steal and went in for the lay-up, slid past everybody, and scored on a drive. All of a sudden, they're up 12–2. We caught up with a spurt of our own, and then it was back and forth, back and forth. Usually just a run-and-gun, one-on-one team, the Bullets were playing play-off defense now, too. They were up tight on us, diving for loose balls, doubling up and trying to get in the passing lanes. With Willis on the bench late in the second quarter, Earl led a Bullet spurt, which gave them a 6-point halftime lead.

We played a little tougher defense in the third period, and went into the fourth quarter up by 3. Earl was keeping them in the game. He was spinning and reversing, and shaking and baking, even though I had my hand in his face all the time. He was shooting the ball from under his hip and behind his ear. I was all over him, and he was still making some incredible shots. Players have scored more points on me than Earl was doing now—West had, earlier in the season—but I don't think anyone ever did it like Earl. West got his points in the flow of the game. Earl was doing it one-on-one.

There was less than a minute to play in regulation time when Earl came down, twisted around, put up a fadeaway, and scored. The Bullets were on top, 101–100. We missed at the other end, and the Bullets got the ball back. There were only about thirty seconds left, so Red told us to foul, and Barnett did. Earl made one from the line to put them up by two. Bradley tied it up with a drive. Now, Earl, who had scored the Bullets' last 8 points in a row, got ready to bring the ball upcourt with just 24 seconds to go. Before he took the in-bounds pass, he asked me what the score was. I think Earl is nearsighted and couldn't see the scoreboard very well.

"You're leading, man," I told him. "You guys are up." They weren't, of course, and I figured, Maybe he'll take it easy if he thinks they are. You gotta take any advantage you can find.

As Earl reached the front court, Barnett tried to come over to double him, but Earl got away and moved to the top of the key. He leaned back into me. I was tight on him, not sending him right or left, not overplaying him either way. I just wanted to keep him right in front of me. When he acted, I reacted. He turned sideways and gave me a head fake, and then went up to shoot. I went up with him, not trying so much to block the shot, just trying to distract him a little, get him to move it by a fraction of an inch. Right before the buzzer went off, the shot missed. We were going to overtime.

Baltimore took the lead in the extra period. With around a minute left, they were still up, and they had the ball. Kevin Loughery, a quick-draw shooter, was open for a twenty-footer, which could just about clinch it for them. He missed. We got the rebound, went down the court, and cut the lead to two points. Again it was Earl's ball. I was thinking, Steal now, although I'd only had a couple of them all game. I hadn't been looking to make any steals early on because a steal wouldn't have made much difference then. That's the time when I'm like a boxer in the early rounds, stalking my man, feeling him out. Even when I think I can steal the ball early in the game, I try to lay off. I want to save it for when it's important. I want to lull my man, get him comfortable, make him feel he has nothing to worry about from me. I wanted Earl to continue to bring the ball up at the end the way he'd been bringing it up all game.

I didn't look at Earl's face. I only watched his waist, and his legs. Wherever his waist went, he had to go. I watched how he dribbled, trying to get the rhythm of the bounce, the cadence he was using. Trying to steal at that point, I knew, was a risk. If I went for the ball and missed, Earl would go right by me for an easy basket. I may have known it, but I didn't even consider it. If you're going to be the best, you have to take the risks. They didn't even seem like risks; they were the only way to play.

Earl got near the top of the key again. I crouched down even lower and flicked out with my right hand, my stealing hand, and just got enough of the ball to knock it away from Earl. Barnett was waiting, picked the ball up, and went downcourt to lay it in. Just as he was about to score, there was a foul. On the line, Rich was cool: The two free throws tied the score.

There were twenty-three seconds left, and oh, man, there was Earl again, bringing the ball up one more time.

He moved left to right this time, with his back to me. Normally, he dribbled with his right hand, because that was the way he liked to make his spin move. This time, though, it was in his left hand, and that meant the ball was behind a little, and just a bit easier to steal. I went to the back, almost behind him, and slapped at the ball again, and got it rolling to Barnett. Rich picked it up and headed to the Baltimore hoop, with Mad Dog Carter, who ran like a sprinter, chasing him. Barnett was left-handed and not ambidextrous, and damn, he was on the right side of the court. That meant he had to slow down maybe a fraction of a second to get the right angle for the lay-up. That gave Carter, who can really jump, enough time. He went up and blocked it—except to me, and to Red, and to all the Knicks and all the 19,500 Knick fans, it was goaltending. No question. He got it on the way down.

Red and Willis argued the call, but I didn't say a word. I figured it all evens out in the end. A lot of times when I go up for my shot, I don't get fouled and I get the call. How can I bitch when I don't get it? Or when I get called for a foul I didn't commit? And then why get all excited over something I can't change and something I can't control? With the exception of Mendy Rudolph, I didn't even know the names of any of the refs. Some of the players would get all bent out of shape when they saw that a certain ref was going to be officiating that night. In the locker room before we went out on the floor, Phil Jackson would get extremely upset as soon as he heard that one particular ref would be working the game. He'd keep shaking his head back and forth. "I can't believe this guy is reffing tonight," Phil would start complaining. "I mean, the guy's a menace. A zero. Every time I move, he's calling something on me." Right away, a half hour before the tip-off, Phil was already psyched. And the way it would work out, he'd play tentatively, not doing things the way he normally would, waiting for the guy to make a bad call against him. That wasn't my game. I didn't care who called it, I played the same.

Even when I was a kid, I never complained to the refs. Maybe it was inherited. While my mother could be emotional, my father had always been an extremely calm person, always with his wits about him. I never saw him upset. No matter what my mother or I or the other kids ever did, I never saw him lose his cool. Almost nothing seemed to bother him very much. Except for my family and sometimes for sports, I was the same way. I never cared that much about anything to let it get me upset. If someone took my girlfriend, I might be bothered for a little bit of time, but I would get over it.

Arguing with the refs also wasn't the way I was brought up. George Coffee, one of my high school coaches, once told me, "Don't ever lose your head, son. Your brains are in it." From grade school through college, I had always been the captain of the team, whatever sport it was. I was always told that I had to keep the team together, I had to be cool when everybody else was hot. I remember when we played for the city football championship. With under two minutes to go, we were losing, and everyone in the huddle was talking and nervous and excited, except for me. In a situation like that, you are supposed to look to the sidelines, where the coach is supposed to be sending in the plays. But when I looked, the coach had panicked, too. There were no plays coming in. I told the guys, "Shut up, everybody," and the huddle became so quiet you could hear a pin drop. Everyone looked at me, and waited for me to tell them what to do. I told the linemen that we'd run a quarterback sneak, and that "you had all better get me in the end zone." They did, and we ended up winning the game and the championship. Afterward, the coaches congratulated me on controlling things and being so cool about it. It paid, I realized, to control my emotions.

During a game, I might have been boiling inside, but I'd keep the emotions under the surface and under control. Later, I'd let them out. In high school, when we lost a game, I cried. When we'd lost to the Celtics in the play-offs the season before, I was a grown man, but I cried again. Just not in front of anybody else. I know I can't play well when I'm upset and let my emotions get to me and let them be seen by everybody. Very few players can perform well when they're angry. The only one I ever saw who got better when he was upset was Earl Monroe. When he got mad at a referee, he took it out on the other team, like he wanted to show them he didn't need the good calls or something. That wasn't the way it worked for me. In twelve years in the NBA, I never got a technical. I don't think there's any other ballplayer who played so many years and put in so many minutes at such a high level who can say that.

Mendy Rudolph stuck with his call: It was a clean block and we went into a second overtime.

In the second five minutes, we took a quick lead until the

Bullets came back and tied it up at 117 apiece, the twenty-third time the game had been tied. We had the ball with fifty-two seconds to go and called a play for Bradley, who was supposed to come off a DeBusschere pick and get the ball by the free-throw line. Marin was right on Dollar, so Willis broke down the lane with Gus Johnson right behind him. Gus went for my pass but was a little late, and Willis laid it in for the lead. With eighteen seconds to go, Earl tried it one final time, but he was spent. He forced a jumper, which missed. Unseld came down with the rebound, and he missed, too. Willis finally got it and the Butcher sealed it with a free throw.

It seemed like we had played forever. In the locker room, I asked somebody, "Hey, how many overtimes were there?" Earl got 39 points. When it counted though, I had stopped him. In one of the newspapers the next day, the headline was: MONROE WINS THE BATTLE, FRAZIER WINS THE WAR. I liked that.

The Bullets had played well and gotten great games from Earl and from Mad Dog Carter, and we hadn't played our best. I had hit only a third of my shots and scored just 11 points. From the beginning, I wasn't hitting, and so I hadn't even looked too much for my shots. I tried to do other things—rebound, pass the ball, concentrate on defense. And there was a lot of defense to concentrate on. Still, the guys wouldn't let me forget my poor shooting. "Hey, man,"

Willis said, "I saw your jump shot down in Florida. Somebody said it was on the beach, making its way real slow up north. When you think it's gonna get here?" Yet even with my problems, we had won anyway. Over the last two seasons, we had done it to Baltimore again and again. All of New York had. The Mets had done it to the Orioles, and the Jets put it to the Colts. A man could start to believe in fate right around here. We'd never say it out loud, but we had the attitude that if we could keep the game close, we'd find a way to beat the Bullets. We felt we were better than they were when the game was on the line. We had done it so many times in the past, they had to be psyched about it. We didn't worry if we'd get down by 10–15 to them. We knew we'd maintain our poise and come back. They had to know it, too.

Baltimore was a carnival. I liked to play there. It was exciting. The people cared about their basketball and knew how to put on a show. As I walked from the Holiday Inn to the Civic Center, which was right in downtown, the locals got on my case. "Hey, Frazier, the Pearl's goin' to get fifty on you tonight." "He gonna spin on you tonight, Clyde." "The Pearl will be shining."

A wildly dressed dude, supposedly a friend of Earl's and nicknamed Dancing Harry, was at the arena. He was like the Bullets unofficial cheerleader, dancing by himself alongside the court and giving the evil eye to the visiting team. He was doing his crazy steps, ragging the Knicks, and egging on the crowd. He better stay away from Willis, I thought. One time, the captain found Harry in the corridor right outside our locker room, and he was going to kick his butt from Baltimore down to Washington.

Rock music blared from the loudspeakers. The Bullets came out, and their entire lineup did a dunk routine to the beat. The biggest cheer went to Gus Johnson, who really was the first of the NBA's high flyers. Gus zoomed through the air like a rocket with muscles, and then slammed it one-handed. Pretty impressive. I wasn't supposed to look, but I saw it all out of the corner of my eye, and it was quite a show. I wasn't sure everybody on our team *could* dunk.

Once again, the Bullets got off early and we were sluggish, like we were still overwhelmed by the dunk show. With four minutes still to go in the third period, they had a 9-point lead when Riordan came in for Barnett. Dick had been guarding Earl, and I knew more than anybody what a tiring job that was. He was beat. We went into the final period down by 6 when Mike took the tap-off and drove straight in for a lay-up. That was why Riordan was a great driver: He took the shortest route to the hoop. If somebody happened to be in the way, hey, that wasn't Mike's problem.

The basket was so aggressive, we had taken it to the Bullets so directly, it seemed to ignite us behind Riordan. Mike continued to score and was really harassing Earl, forcing him out farther than he wanted to be, getting his hand in Earl's face every time he went up.

Monroe got only one free throw in the quarter, and we took a 4-point lead with under a minute and a half to go. The ball was ours, but the twenty-four-second clock was running down. With time about to expire, Bradley shot a prayer from deep in the corner. The ball hit the side of the backboard as the buzzer went off. It bounced a few times with none of the Bullets going for it. I didn't, either. I figured it was Baltimore's ball, since the shot didn't hit the rim before time was up. I guessed the Bullets thought so, too. Shows you how much all of us professionals know. The ball didn't have to touch the rim to reset the clock. It was enough if it touched *any* part of the backboard or the rim.

It must take a Princeton man to know that. With nobody else moving, Bradley snuck in for the rebound, and we got another twenty-four seconds. I love an Ivy League education. This second time, with the clock running down, Dollar shot an airball, not touching even the side of anything. For a split-second, Unseld had the rebound, until DeBusschere spiked it out of his hands. Willis grabbed it back, though, and put it up and in just at the twenty-four-second buzzer. I felt like we were a cat with several lives. With our last life, we pulled away to a 7-point win.

We were ahead in the series 2–0 now, we were confident, and really, there shouldn't have been any major worries for us. There was a blip, though, forming on the horizon. Willis's right knee, which had been hurting him for a long time, was getting worse. Willis didn't mention it, but after we returned to New York, he didn't practice with the team. When I saw him run a little, he limped, and in the trainer's room, I saw him get a shot of cortisone.

Well, Willis was always hurting, from one thing or another. But he almost never complained about it, and we all figured he'd be there when the time came. He would answer the bell.

The third game was on Easter Sunday. Because it was an afternoon game, on national television, I couldn't go to church for the holiday. I should have felt bad about that. Growing up, I had been a religious person. Even though my mother never made us go, in high school I went every Sunday on my own. I liked going. I liked the preacher and I liked the singing and I liked the way it made me feel. Going to church did something good for my soul. I'd feel cleansed when I came out of church. When I went off to college, I started moving away from it. I guess I thought I had more important things to do. When I came to the NBA, I went even less, almost not at all. It's tough to be religious when you're a professional ballplayer. In the locker room, every other word is a curse word, and the only time you ever hear God's name is when a damn is attached. Your life is so caught up with playing and practicing and playing some more that you're not much concerned with anything that doesn't bear directly on the game. You feel your body can do anything you want it to, and so what you want to do is feed the body, not the soul. And then, too, there's no time, or at least you think there isn't. There are games on Sunday, and that's a good excuse. Of course there's time enough to go to church if a player really wants to, but most never take the time. I think Cazzie was the only really religious guy on the Knicks, or at least the only one who talked about it. And that was another thing: No one liked to be thought of as a guy who took something too seriously. Other than basket-ball, that is. So I was occupied with other things.

One night in the mid-seventies, I was at a discotheque talking to two girls I had never seen before. Out of nowhere, I asked them if they knew a good church to go to. All of a sudden, I found myself wanting to get back into the church. The girls said Canaan Baptist up in Harlem was a good one, and the next morning I went up there. I went late, because I didn't want to be there with a lot of people who might rec-ognize me. As soon as I arrived, I felt comfortable. This was where I had been, this was where I should be. Something, I realized when I walked in, had been missing from my life, and this was it; this was a way of bringing God back into my life.

From then on, I've attended church every Sunday.

Wherever I am, whatever city, I go. I'm not a preacher or any kind of evangelist. I don't broadcast my beliefs, and I don't tell others what's right for them. I know, too, that going to church doesn't make me a better person, just by itself, but it makes me *feel* like a better person, and reinforces my ideas about what I should do to become a better person.

I came to understand that I had always been a taker and not a giver. Through the church, I've learned how to give. Sometimes it can be money. When I was playing and taking down a good salary, I never gave the church two dollars. Now I give each week, and the more money I make, the more I give back. It also doesn't have to be money. I work with kids now and make speeches about drugs and alcohol and I give clinics, because that's also giving back.

It was obvious from the start of game three that Willis was having trouble. He was moving slower than usual, laboring. Still, we held on throughout the first two periods, even leading by one at the half. In the third quarter—and that was our time, man, when *we* used to blow teams away— things fell apart for us. We were not shooting well or handling the ball smoothly. We missed nine of our first ten shots in the half, while the Bullets, behind Earl, Loughery, and Marin, made six of their first seven. They were suddenly up by nine, and we were fading.

Everything we threw up was off, and Unseld was there to clear the boards. He completely dominated Willis. On both the offensive and defensive glass, he was like a vacuum cleaner. He went up and grabbed everything with two hands, snatching the ball like a soccer goalie. Sometimes he plucked the ball out of the air with the two hands, wheeled around, and threw a bullet pass to Earl at midcourt, all before he came down.

The Bullets won it easily. For the game, Willis got 5 boards, the Knicks got a total of 30, and Unseld, all by himself, took down 34. Unseld outrebounded our entire team. I couldn't believe it. He was a great rebounder, but I'd never seen that before, not in high school or college, not one guy outrebounding an entire team.

Even though Unseld could jump, he did it mainly with positioning. He had a great awareness of where the ball would go. He knew how to time his jump. He was also very, very strong. One time back in college, his Louisville team came to Carbondale to play Southern Illinois. Halfway through the game, one of our guys, who was about 6′ 4″, blocked a shot on Unseld and smacked the ball right off Wes's forehead. Wes was angry. He got the ball back and almost tore the gym down he dunked the ball so hard.

Unseld knew his job with the Bullets. With the exception sometimes of Gus Johnson, he was the Bullets' only rebounder. He'd be alone under the basket while all the other guys would race down the court and wait for his outlet pass so they could score. Unseld was extremely unselfish, and never looked to score himself. I would have loved to play with him; I could've gotten a lot more shots.

Game three was a humiliating kind of loss, and yet it was also the best kind of thing that could happen to us. When you lose the way we did, you can't wait until the next game. Our pride had been wounded, and we wanted to get back at them. We knew we were much better than we had played. We needed to redeem ourselves.

Pride, though, wasn't enough to stop Earl. Back in Baltimore, the Bullets blew us away again in the third period. Monroe didn't even seem to be looking at the basket, and then, boom, he'd score. We made a run at them in the fourth quarter and made it close. Then, twice in the last two minutes, Earl isolated himself on the right side, let the clock run down, and then drilled a twenty-five-footer. Baltimore tied the series at two games each.

A little more than a year later, I read in the newspaper one morning that the Knicks had traded Mike Riordan and Dave Stallworth to the Bullets for Earl Monroe. It didn't make any sense. Earl *was* the Bullets. He epitomized their whole one-on-one, fast-breaking style. I thought they would never give him up. And I couldn't conceive of Earl being with the Knicks. He was the complete opposite of everything we stood for—teamwork, patience, control. We also didn't need another guard, especially not one who had been used to handling the ball all the time. That meant I had to be expendable. I thought for sure the Knicks would be trading me. The press wrote that Frazier and Monroe could never play together because we would need two balls. I wondered about it.

After a couple of practices, I didn't wonder anymore. When training camp opened for the next season, Earl made the sacrifices, not me. Very quiet and almost an introvert off the court, Earl was willing to give up his flashy on-the-court personality. He sacrificed because he wanted to win. He toned down his game, while I played the same way I always had. He played defense and rebounded and hit the open man, which he had never done before, because the Bullets had never asked him to. One ball was enough for us.

I think it helped Earl that he saw he didn't have to do it all by himself anymore. Some players can't handle that; if they can't control the game the way they're used to, they don't want to play at all. But when we played together, Earl seemed happy scoring 18 or 20 a game instead of 25, because we were winning, and he knew that if he had an off-night, it wasn't going to kill us—the way it might've killed the Bullets. When we were in the backcourt, if I was hot, Earl was willing to get me the ball. If he was hot, I'd get it to him. There were times, of course, when Earl could still do his Pearl number, spinning and bumping and bobbing his head and throwing it in from nowhere. But he could save those times now for when we really needed him to go one-on-one, rather than having to do it for forty minutes.

Even before he came to the Knicks, Earl and I were friends, although we had never really spoken much to each other or hung out together when he was with the Bullets— or for that matter, after the trade, either. But we were friends, I think, out of mutual respect for each other. We had been enemies on the court, and neither of us ever gave any quarter. And we admired that about each other. Earl knew that if he scored 30 on me, he had to earn every one of them. I knew that he was going to make me work harder than anybody else in basketball. We never hung out much together because Earl is an extremely private person, very reserved, and not at all like I thought he would be from the way he played. The funny thing is, I probably see him more now socially than I did when we were playing together. He lives only a few blocks away from me on the Upper West Side of Manhattan, and we've done a number of appearances together. When he needs me, like for a fund-raising tennis clinic he runs, I'm there, just like he was with me for six seasons in the Knicks' backcourt.

At a practice before game five, I was alone in the locker room bathroom, sitting at the mirror combing my hair, when Red came in.

"Clyde," he said, "Monroe is killing us. Do you think you can stop him?"

"Red, what the hell do you think I've been trying to do? I know what deodorant he wears. I can tell you the label on his jock. I'm trying, you know. What else can I do?"

"Listen, from now on, I want you to concentrate on defense. Forget about offense. Don't worry about scoring. We don't need your points. Just play defense and move the team. Concentrate on Monroe, contain him. Just stop the son of a bitch."

In the locker room before game five, I knew we were ready. I could sense it. Everybody was quiet, very laid-back, no rah-rah stuff at all. Nobody said, "When does this fracas start?" This was serious now. We put our hands in, Red and Danny and everyone, and held them there, maybe just a split-second longer than usual.

During the warm-ups, I didn't see Willis limping any-more. He was moving easily, without any real difficulty. A couple of days earlier, he had gotten a second cortisone shot for the knee. Now he was jumping higher and didn't seem to be in any pain. I didn't know if it was the cortisone, but I knew that we needed more from our captain. We had played the Bullets four games, and Unseld had outplayed Willis in all four. We couldn't win it if that went on.

When the game started, though, it looked like Willis's pride hurt more than his knees. He finally seemed physically able to do the things he normally did. From the opening tap, there was fire in his eyes. The man was unstoppable. He hit hook shots, jumpers, slam-dunks, drivers, you name it. Oh, man, it was a joy to watch him play like that. I almost wanted to step back and watch it. I hadn't seen him move that well since the play-offs the year before. This was the Willis that used to be, the Willis that could have been all the time if injuries hadn't cut him down.

When Willis played like this, it made it so much easier for the rest of us. With him completely dominating Unseld at both ends of the court, Earl wasn't able to be involved as much in the Bullets' offense. He couldn't get the ball where he wanted it, out on the break, without Unseld getting it for him off the boards. He seemed out of sync, and missed two thirds of his shots. I was able to hold him to 18 points, which was almost like shutting Earl out.

Willis intimidated all of the Bullets, including Earl. I didn't normally see the big guys play defense, because my back was usually to them. So I didn't have any idea what they were doing—or not doing—under the basket. Later, when I watched the film of game five, I realized, maybe for the first time, how great a player Willis Reed was, and how I was not as great a defensive player as I thought. When guys got past me, Willis was there, rejecting their shots. If he didn't block them, he was causing them to shoot high, or off to the left, or a bit to the right. Watching him save my butt made me a lot more humble about my defensive skills.

With the exception of Willis, none of us shot very well, but it didn't matter. Willis put in 36 points and took down 36 rebounds, all by himself. Our defense, particularly in the third period, did the rest, and we won it, 101–80. Our lead was 3–2 in games.

We were supposed to do it with defense, but the Bullets, when they wanted to, could play pretty good defense, too. For most of game six back in Baltimore, Mad Dog Carter was on me. It was like playing against a guy on a trampoline. He jumped all over the place, he dived for loose balls, and he never let go of me. Sometimes, Gus Johnson switched over on me, and going against him was like playing a brick wall. Gus hand checked all the time, and I couldn't slap his hand away. I had his fingerprints all over me, on my thighs and my waist. There was no way I could drive against him.

With both teams playing tough defense, neither club was able to shoot well in the first half, and here was the damn third quarter again. Earl and Gus and the whole Bullet team started to come on strong. The Butcher had four fouls and Gus took it right to him, scoring the first three baskets of the half. Then it was Earl's turn, scoring 5 straight points, and we could never catch up. With DeBusschere and Bradley both on the bench for a long time, we were forced to play the Baltimore kind of game, one-on-one, and there was no way we were going to beat them at that. Cazzie and Stalls came off the bench to get us some points, but our big guys,

Willis, Dave, and Bill, made just five of their thirty-four shots. The final score was 96–87, Bullets, and there was going to be a game seven.

It was a subdued locker room after the game. When we should have been up, where we could have had one of our biggest victories of the year, we had played badly. We had let them off the hook, and I think we were annoyed at ourselves for that. The great teams of the past, like the Celtics, if they had a team down, would stomp them away. The Butcher, who sat out most of the game in foul trouble, was angry at Red for keeping him on the bench. I was upset, too, because I didn't think I was getting enough help on Earl. We were supposed to be playing team defense, but sometimes Earl would dribble right past guys, and they weren't picking him up. They should have been doubling him more. I just stared down at the floor, realizing that if we were going to stop Earl and win this thing, it would depend on me. I'd have to stop him by myself.

Game seven would be back at the Garden. Hallelujah, man. There is definitely a home-court advantage. Maybe it wasn't as great an advantage back then as it is now. Today, almost everybody wins almost all the time at home. Back then, it wasn't such a sure thing. A lot of our eighteen straight wins had come on the road. In a lot of cities, the crowds didn't show much enthusiasm, and that's the real edge, what the crowd does. The Knicks had the advantage because of the New York fans. When the crowd would start yelling, "Defense, defense," it would pump us up. It wasn't something that was choreographed, the way they do today with football players waving flags and all, trying to get the fans into a game. It was a natural happening. When the Garden crowd was roaring, it could shake up the other team, and the refs, too. It's a close call in a key situation, and the ref hears almost twenty thousand people screaming at him. Suddenly, he's giving the ball to us, even if it was obvious that it went off the other team. When the ref is undecided, you better believe the crowd influences him.

I was nervous all day before game seven. When I ate my meal down at the hotel restaurant, I kept dropping my knife and fork, and even the salt and pepper. When we came out for the warm-ups, the ball kept slipping out of my hands, and I couldn't hit the side of the moon. Right before we went out, the locker room was as quiet as I ever remembered it. Before we went out, Red told me he wanted Barnett to bring the ball up, so I could save my energy and concentrate on stopping Earl. I was not going to shoot. I was not going to handle the ball. Just stop Earl. That's all I had to do.

The fans started screaming and clapping before the organist could even get close to finishing the national anthem. They couldn't wait, and it looked like neither could we. For the first time in the series—really for the first time in over a month—we exploded. Dave and Dick were taking it to the hoop, and Cazzie came off the bench to give us a lift. Earl got his points, but not when they counted, and he had to work awfully hard for them. We were up by 15 at the half, and never let the Bullets make too much of a run at us. The final score was 127–114.

I sat drained in front of my cubicle. The Bullets had run us up and down the court for two weeks. I was absolutely exhausted, but relieved. The season wasn't over yet.

CHAPTER

8

WHILE BALTIMORE WAS PUSHING US TO THE LIMIT, Milwaukee had it easy with Philadelphia, taking them out in five games. They were rested and we were tired. They had no injuries and we were a little beaten up. Still, I almost looked forward to playing them, at least in comparison to going up against Baltimore again. The Bucks weren't as frightening. They were a methodical team, coming down and setting up, then looking for Alcindor down low. Their game was better suited to us, because we liked that kind of half-court game, too.

The Bullets had five or maybe six guys who could go off at any time and were capable of blowing us out. Milwaukee, we felt, only had two: Alcindor and a guard named Flynn Robinson. We didn't think the rest of their starters, Jon McGlocklin in the backcourt and Greg Smith and Bobby Dandridge up front, could kill us if we had to lay off them.

Robinson was a great outside shooter who could light it

up from downtown. In a preseason game, he had burned us for over 40. He was strong and a good driver. He had the moves. He just didn't like contact. Normally I guarded him during the regular season, and I had always stayed off him. On defense, I don't like contact, either; my game was surprise. I didn't want to touch my man and let him know where I was. I wanted to keep him guessing. If he didn't know where I was coming from, he could turn the wrong way and I could flick the ball away from the backside. A few times during a game I might touch, using it for the psychological effect. It gave me another element of surprise. In the Baltimore series, Monroe had always tried to bump and grind with me. He loved contact, because if he had a body on him, he always knew which way to spin.

Robinson was different. In a game near the end of the regular season, I was on the bench when Barnett was defending against him. Rich had his hand on Robinson's hip, and Robinson kept trying to slap it away. He got more and more annoyed as Barnett would put his hand back and continued to bump him all over the place. That was the way Barnett played defense. Robinson wasn't happy, and he was complaining to the refs, and all of a sudden he forgot about what he was supposed to be doing out there. He started shooting airballs and just standing around, not wanting the ball anymore. Hey, I thought, maybe this is the way I should guard the guy.

If I played him physically, I felt I could stop Robinson, or at least hold him down. Alcindor was a different case. He always was. There were two strategies. We could try to help out Willis as much as possible, double- and triple-teaming Lew whenever he got the ball. Or we could let him get his points and try to stop the other guys, smother them completely. The Bucks were an expansion team and had a lot of rookies, and we figured they'd make rookie mistakes. As we headed into the series, our strategy was to contain the other guys as best we could, but to make sure we helped out Willis with Alcindor.

Lew was so difficult to defend and to double because, unlike most other centers, he didn't put the ball on the floor very much. Most of the big guys, they get the ball, put it down, and we could swipe at it. But Alcindor was used to guys swiping at him from college—and probably from high school, too. He'd always had guys swarming around him, and he was aware when a double- or triple-team was coming. The Bucks' idea was to isolate him one-on-one with Willis, preferably on the left side of the court, so he could shoot the sky hook. We had to get in his way, harass him, and not let him work alone on Willis.

From the first minute of game one, I had my hand on Robinson. He was not a great ballhandler, and I tried to force him to the sides of the court, where Barnett could come over to apply pressure. He wanted to go to the right, but I was a step over to that direction because I wanted to make him go to his left. Always force them to their weaker side. Robinson got an annoyed look on his face. He tried to slap my hand away again and again. He was spending so much time doing that, he wasn't concentrating on what he should have been doing. When he slapped, he couldn't be penetrating, and he couldn't be shooting well from the outside.

Alcindor got his points, 35 of them, but I held Robinson without a field goal in the first half and to 4-of-16 shooting for the game. As we expected, the other Bucks couldn't pick it up. We were up by 16 going into the last 5 minutes and won by 8. We were ahead in the series, 1–0.

It shouldn't mean anything for game two. I figured they had pride the way we had. We got blown out and I got embarrassed, and I figured, Hey, it's payback time. It'll probably be the same way for Robinson.

It wasn't. In game two, Robinson got only one more bucket than he did in game one. Each time he got the ball it was like he wanted to shoot it as soon as possible, so I'd get off him. As we ran upcourt, he was complaining to the ref, "Man, the guy's fouling me. He's all over me. You gotta call something." I didn't say a word.

It's a team game. *We* had to beat *them*. But the play-offs are also personal. Matchup time. That's what the press focuses on. If, say, Greg Smith has a big game, the press writes that he beat Bradley, it's Dollar's fault. The real reason might be that Bill was helping out so much on Lew and nobody picked up on his man. Still, game two was as personal as you get, a duel at the O.K. Corral between Alcindor and Reed. Willis physically beat the hell out of Lew, pushing and shoving him, and the rest of us swiped at the ball every time he put it on the floor. It didn't seem to help very much. Lew dunked, he drove around Willis, he skied over him. When we all converged on him to help, he threw the ball back out for easy Bucks baskets. At the other end of the court, Willis wasn't giving an inch. He shot the jumper even though Lew came out and had his hand in Willis's face. Reed drove, he fought on the boards and put the ball back in.

It was tight all the way. With fifty-two seconds to go, we were up by one when Lew wheeled for the hoop. Reed, tired and maybe just a step slower than he was earlier, fouled him. It was Willis's fifth foul. Alcindor went to the line for two, with a chance to put the Bucks ahead. As always, he seemed nonchalant about what he had to do and showed no emotion. I couldn't see anything at all on his face. There was no way to tell if he was nervous. This time, though, he shot the first one and made a face when he missed it. He missed the second one, too.

Willis got the rebound. After we ran some time off the clock, the Butcher missed a jumper, but Cazzie came down with the ball this time, and was pushed by Freddie Crawford. Cazzie made both of his shots, and the Bucks couldn't catch us. We won by one, to go up two games to none in the series. Lew scored 38 points, got 23 rebounds, and even passed off for 11 assists. Still, he had missed the 2 points they had to have. Tough. There's no place for sympathy in the play-offs. Willis, who had 36 points and 18 rebounds himself, had gotten the crucial rebound. He'd won the duel. In the end, the only thing that matters is the result.

We had gotten up on the Bullets and then let them off the hook. We had to go to Milwaukee now to play the next two games, and we knew we had to win at least one of them. If we didn't, we'd be letting them right back into it. With the home crowd behind them and the Dixieland band playing for them, they would be ready.

When the introductions for game three were made, Flynn Robinson, the captain of the Bucks, wasn't in the starting lineup. Oh, boy, I thought. The Bucks were saying that I had literally taken Robinson out of the game. With me in there, they couldn't have him on the floor. It made me feel terrific. My confidence soared.

Robinson was replaced by Crawford, an old friend from my rookie year with the Knicks. Freddie couldn't shoot from the outside like Robinson, but he was tough and drove well to the hoop, and he didn't back down. With him in there, the Bucks got off fast. Even though we knew what we had to do coming in, we were flat. Knowing what you have to do sometimes isn't enough. It was hard always to translate that into what was in the gut. You'd tell yourself, Hey, man, we can put them away tonight, we can just about close out the series, but the gut knew, I guess, that we still had other chances to do it. We *thought* we were putting out as hard as we could, but maybe there wasn't that intensity we had when our backs really were to the wall.

Milwaukee was up by 16 in the third quarter, when we finally started to get that intensity. It began when Red told us to put on the press; there is no way you can press if you aren't intense. The Bucks couldn't handle the all-court defense. They had no real ballhandlers on the court, no one to calm them down and keep them playing their game. Larry Costello, the Milwaukee coach, had to bring in Guy Rodgers, who was at the end of his career and didn't play very much anymore, just to help them get the ball up the court.

Still, the Bucks had Alcindor. He was overwhelming Willis, and with Bobby Dandridge and Crawford doing enough damage for the Bucks to hold on, they ended up winning it by 5. That cut our series lead to 2–1, the same script we had followed in the Baltimore series. Yet somehow, the loss didn't hurt as much as when the Bullets beat us. Sometimes you lost and you could live with it. Yeah, the bottom line was the W, but when we played so bad for so much of the game, we could just forget about it. Sitting in the locker room after the game, we knew we couldn't play much worse. The Bucks had dominated us, and still, they only won by 5. And now, maybe, we had gotten that kind of lethargic game out of our systems.

It was obvious to everybody: Game four was the most important game of the series. This was the pivot. If they won, we'd be all even, and they'd have the confidence and the momentum. If we took it, we'd be up by two and would still have two more games left to play in New York.

There are times when you just know you're not going to get beat. You feel sure things are going to go your way. Just before the buzzer went off to end the first half of game four, the Rave threw the ball to the basket from about forty-five feet away. *Bang.* It was dead center on target, giving us a 20-point lead as we ran off the court. After completely dominating them in the first half, during the break we were all loose and confident in the locker room. Still, I figured they were going to make a run at us, and in the third quarter, they did.

By the time Red called a time-out, they had the lead down to 13. "You gotta see the ball, dammit, see the ball," Red told us, like maybe he hadn't been saying it all season. I saw the ball, and all I saw was that it was still going in for them and not for us. The Bucks cut it down to 7, and then

Willis got his fourth foul. The Bucks kept coming, scoring a total of 16 points in a row, and with 5 minutes left in the period, they cut the lead down to 2.

I was angry bringing the ball upcourt. It should never have been this close. We should have buried them. Near the top of the key, I saw Cazzie rolling to me from the corner. This was my job. Get Cazzie the ball. I did, and he popped it straight in from twenty feet. We were up by four, and more important, we'd broken their string. Alcindor got a dunk back at the other end, but didn't see the ball much after that. We tightened up the defense, and the Bucks weren't able to get it into him. This is what happens to a young team. Instead of their main man taking the shots at crunch time, McGlocklin and Robinson, who was 4-for-18 from the floor, put it up, and missed. Not Cazzie, though. He was on a Russell roll. The momentum had turned around. Milwaukee made another small run at us before the end of the quarter, to cut it again to 3 points, but they'd blown their load. We'd weathered it. We'd taken their best shot and were still breathing, and still in the lead. Behind Cazzie, we pulled away in the fourth quarter to win by 9 and go up 3–1 in games.

"Hey, man," Barnett said in the locker room, "they can phone it in now. No need for them even to show up. Maybe they send us a telegram from Western Union." We all knew that the series was over. We were going back to New York, and even if we didn't win the next one, they'd still have to beat us in Milwaukee and one more time back at the Garden. No way they would be able to do that. No question.

The Bucks didn't look beaten when they came out for game five. I couldn't see anything in their eyes, or the way they moved. But that was the way they played, like they were already planning their summer vacations. They couldn't hold on to the ball, and their passes were coming closer to us than to them. Barnett got hot early on, and by the end of the first quarter, we were up by 16. A few minutes into the second period, Larry Costello took Robinson out after he missed another shot. He never put him in again. I scored only 2 points in the game. Didn't matter to me. I knew I'd done my job.

The game was like a teaching film, the kind of thing high school coaches would show to their kids. All the plays we'd practiced all year, the Barry and 22 and Celtics, worked perfectly. Everything was working. We were up by 24 at the half, and this time we didn't let up in the third quarter. The defense forced the Bucks into turnover after turnover, and then we converted at our end. Late in the period, when the lead had reached around 30, Costello took Lew out of the game. He was conceding that we'd won it. The fans in the Garden started chanting, "Good-bye, Lewie, good-bye, Lewie, we hate to see you go." Fans are really something. The man had just had a monster series and done everything he could do for his team to win. And they were making fun of him. It was cruel. It wasn't Lew's fault that he didn't wind up playing ball back in his hometown of New York. It wasn't his fault that he was tall and talented. I guess it was a way for the fans who weren't tall and talented to cut him down to size. But that didn't make it nice.

The final score was 132–96, and we became the official Eastern Division champions. There was just one more step to go.

CHAPTER

9

IT WAS HARD TO THINK ABOUT MAYBE PLAYING seven more games. It was the end of April by now, and I'd be glad when all this was over. It was time to have some fun already. I had been killing myself for eight months now, and I was getting just a little tired of it. And we still had to play the Lakers.

In the last week of the regular season, Wilt had come back to the Lakers. I wasn't surprised at all: He was a stubborn man. So it was Chamberlain now. And Baylor. And West. Somehow, according to the papers, we were favored for the final round, and *that* surprised me. Look at those guys: at that time, the three greatest play-off scorers in the history of pro basketball. With Wilt back, they had beaten Atlanta in four straight to win the Western Division. They had been to the finals six times in the last ten years. The Knicks hadn't been there once in more than a decade. Yeah, we were favored.

The other guard on the Lakers, the one who played alongside Jerry West, was Dickie Garrett, the only other ex–Southern Illinois Saluki playing in the NBA. I think we had as many players in the finals as any other school. Dickie was a year behind me at SIU, and I knew him pretty well. In practice, we had gone up against each other all the time, and we also played in summer games together. In the days before the final series began, I got telephone calls from a lot of our mutual friends from back at school. "Hey, man, who's going to win it, you or Dickie?" they'd ask me. "You goin' to let Dickie get you, man?" "Some of the guys here think Garrett and the Lakers are gonna put it to you."

I saw Dickie on the Garden court during warm-ups before the start of game one. I didn't talk to players on other teams before, during, or after a game. I didn't want to get friendly with anyone and then have to embarrass him. If I get close to you, I'll feel bad if I show you up. I can't go out and kick your butt as if I don't know who you are. I'll do it anyway, but I'll feel bad about it. Some players can handle those kinds of relationships—not me. This is my business. But Dickie was already an old friend, so we had to say hello to each other.

"What you got going in town, man?" he asked me.

"I don't know. A couple of things. You want to hang out?"

"Sure."

"Okay, see you after, right," I said. Then I got an idea. "Listen, you want to make a bet on this?" I'm not usually a betting man, but with all the guys from college pushing me, it just seemed right.

"Sure."

Garrett had a piece of a nightclub near the Southern Illinois campus. "How about a party back in Carbondale for the winner? Loser pays for it." Like a good rookie who'd learned to do what he's told, Dickie agreed.

Before the game, Red was the same as always. He didn't say anything about how far we'd come, just told us what we had to do tonight, who we'd be guarding. I was going to start on Garrett, not West. Red wanted to keep me out of foul trouble and also give me a chance to free lance and double up on people. Barnett would be on Jerry. Rich played him well. He'd bop West around for forty minutes and really irritate him. Dick had played a couple of seasons with him on the Lakers and practiced with him, and he knew what Jerry liked to do. When Rich was out in L.A., it was always West this, and West that. West was the big star, and everyone, even Baylor and Wilt, came in second. No one paid any attention to Barnett, and if he ever got the ball, it was only as second or third choice. Barnett never said anything about his experiences there, or about West, but I got the feeling he was jealous of Jerry. I think he liked having the chance to show West up.

Red didn't mention anything about testing Wilt and finding out if he could still move and how quick he was after the injury. He didn't have to. We read the papers. We knew we'd have to check him out early, and find out if we could drive on him.

In the first half, Wilt either couldn't move or simply didn't want to. Willis went out first to the corners while Wilt stayed anchored under the basket. Willis scored a few easily and then headed to the foul-line area to try from there. He was hot from there, too, and so Wilt finally came out a little and *whoosh*, Willis drove right by him. That was always Willis's big advantage over the taller centers, his quickness. Wilt was now convinced: no way he was going to come out again. With no one challenging him, Willis started creeping in a little from the area around the line, the rest of us continued to get him the ball, and he stayed hot.

When he did move, Wilt looked slow and lumbering. It seemed to take him a long time to get up in the air. He always used to squat before he'd jump. When you drove on him, you waited for the squat; then, if you timed it right, you could get your shot off. That was the main difference defensively between him and Bill Russell. Russell would stand straight up and you didn't know when he was going to make his move and block your shot. When Wilt wanted to block you, he had to get ready first and set himself. Because of his leg, he didn't seem able to get out of the squat as quickly now. He was still an intimidating presence, and you couldn't just drive down the middle and relax with him around. But we felt we had more time now. By the end of the first half, Willis had 25 points, and we were up by 20 midway through the second period.

Maybe the knee was locking on Wilt. Or maybe, at the age of thirty-three, he was just getting old.

It's funny; I'm forty-three now and I don't feel old. But to a ballplayer, twenty-eight can be old. When you're over thirty, the young players in the league—the guys twenty-two and twenty-three years old—can look at you like you're about to get sent to a home. Some players really hate the feeling of not being young anymore in a young man's game, but getting old as a ballplayer isn't always that bad, if you can accept it. When Willis traded me to Cleveland, I was only thirty-two, but I thought I might retire then. I felt I could still play, but I figured maybe this was the time to get out. I didn't want to wait for my skills to fade away, for me to really be old. I also considered myself a New Yorker: my life was the city, my image was New York, and any place else—particularly Cleveland—would be just a terrible letdown.

After the announcement, I wanted to go down to the Caribbean and get away from thinking about it for a time, but soon afterward, Bill Fitch, the coach, came to New York to talk to me, which made me feel good. He told me he was the guy who made the trade; he wanted me, he needed me there. He thought I would give stability to his young players and would be a leader for them, and I liked that. He wanted me to be a team player and handle the ball and dish it out, and I liked that, too. Little by little, the trade started looking . . . well, not better, but at least acceptable. I decided to go to Ohio.

Cleveland sure wasn't New York. I came there all dressed up, and found there was no place to go. After a game, the few clubs in town were shut down. Restaurants started serving early, and most of them were done by seven or seven-thirty. At midnight, the only thing on television was Flash Gordon. Cleveland didn't swing. Not only weren't there the same things to do as in New York, there wasn't the same exposure either, or even the same weather. I'm not a snow person, and when there's ten inches of it on the ground, I don't want to go anyplace at all, even if there *is* a place to go.

But Cleveland did have one great advantage over New York: I didn't have to be Clyde there, at least not all the time. It wasn't a dangerous environment. I didn't have to live up to any image in Cleveland, even if I could have. I could escape from what the New York public expected of me. If it's up to me to make things happen, the way I had to do in Cleveland, I'm not going to do it. In New York, everything was ready and waiting for me; all I had to do was serve myself.

I could do things in Cleveland that I never did in Manhattan, or never thought I had the time to do. I played cards in Cleveland, and backgammon, and I stayed with the same woman for a whole year. I went to the movies each weekend with the same person. In a sense, it was almost like I was back in college and a family man once again.

I had never really done much reading before I came to Cleveland. During the season, it had been just newspapers and some magazines, and television to watch and the games to play. In the off-seasons, I wanted to take it easy. Whatever energy I expended was directed toward making me the best player I could be. But with the Cavaliers, particularly after I got injured during my first season with them, I finally discovered I had the time, and the interest, to read. I guess, also, I knew my career was going to end, and so I began reading a lot of self-help books to help me with the adjustment to life after basketball. Getting old as a ballplayer forced me to look into things I felt I would need to know once I left the game and was on my own.

I began reading a lot of books about health and diet and yoga and other forms of relaxation. I learned about the dangers of too much red meat and too many desserts and overloading on sugar and caffeine. I started to give them all up. I read books on vocabulary and improving my speech and collections of quotations. I had always been intrigued by quotes, and began to collect them.

I still regret sometimes that I wasn't able to finish my career in New York. It's my adopted city, and I would have liked to leave the game from there, and felt I should have. But in Cleveland I had a chance to get my head on straight. It was sort of a halfway house for me, a place where I started to settle down. I became more of a giver than a taker during my time with the Cavaliers and was able to get my priorities straight.

On the basketball court, however, the two years I spent in Cleveland were awful. I had been playing pretty well when, during the second half of my first season there, I got hurt. I went in for a shot in Chicago, pushed off the side of my foot, and the doctor said I'd be out ten days. It turned out to be a stress fracture, and I missed the rest of the year. My second season, after playing a bit, the foot started to give me trouble again.

I had rarely been injured before, and tried to spend as little time as possible in the trainer's room during my career. But here I was now, at the mercy of my foot. Maybe that's what it meant to get old. It was frustrating, aggravating, and in the end, devastating. I came back again, and started to get into a groove, and then the foot started hurting one more time.

The foot, though, wasn't my only problem. The rest of my body felt fine, physically, but I could tell I was approaching the end. In my second Cleveland training camp, I was missing a lot of shots I thought I should have made. I figured I just had to get in the groove. But I continued to miss those shots. Things weren't flowing the way they used to. I had to work at it harder, which I did. I worked out more intensely than I ever had, to maintain my shape and try to compensate for not being twenty-five anymore. Yeah, I knew my reflexes weren't quite as good as they used to be. A player would make a pass by me and I'd say, Damn, I should've had that ball. A few years ago, I *would've* had that ball. Still, I felt I was better than most guards in the league.

In general, I felt I could still do what I used to. The difference was, I couldn't do it for a long period of time. In the last five minutes of a game, I thought I was as good as ever, but I could no longer be that way over the course of a whole game. The reason wasn't so much physical as mental. My concentration would come and go, and I just couldn't keep my attention on what was happening all game long. In a lot of games, I just got plain bored waltzing the floor the first three quarters. It was like, Hey, man, let me at those last five minutes. That's where it's at. I don't want to go through all this preliminary stuff anymore. I've already *done* it, hundreds of times. Let's get on over to where the game is really won and lost. I never really understood that I wasn't what I used to be. I just realized I was bored.

With my injuries, I became a nonperson to Bill Fitch, who had wanted me to come there so much. If you weren't playing, Fitch wouldn't talk to you. I felt he thought I was dogging it. The relationship got so bad, I dreaded going to the games.

I didn't have to worry. Before I was to report for my third training camp with Cleveland, the Cavaliers released me. It was an emotional release, too, as well as some air being let out of the balloon. I wanted to cry and shout at the same time. I didn't want to sit on the bench a whole year, and I wanted to get on with the rest of my life. But I knew there were things I was going to miss, and twelve years of your life are not easy to just fold up and store away. When a Cleveland front-office man told me, tears almost came to my eyes; but I also wanted to thank him.

I had one more year left on the contract the Cavs had picked up from the Knicks, so they had to pay me anyway. No other team contacted me, so I just said, That's it.

With Wilt not moving, in the second half the Lakers started going more and more to West. Because Barnett had gotten into foul trouble, I was on West now. West could drive as well as shoot from the outside. He was smart and knew how to get behind his picks. He was a good defensive player, and knew how to use Wilt. He'd let you go by him knowing you had to watch out for Wilt, and then he'd come from behind you and block your shot. He had quickness, but most of all, he had the jump shot, that perfect textbook jumper. (I have in my mind, even today, a sharp image of Jerry West: I see that quick step, and then I see him going straight up and floating the easy jumper.) That's what he looked to do first. The key to it was how fast he'd get it off. Even if you were right on him, he'd go up so quickly and have the ball up so high, it was almost impossible to block it. Once he got it going, you had to come up tight on him, and now he was so quick, he could drive by you. Sometimes he might not go all the way to the hoop, but instead take two quick steps and then pull up and shoot. He had you now and you didn't know what the hell to do.

Since he was another right-hander, I took the right side away from him and gave him a step to force him to go left. That meant when he shot, he'd have to bring the ball toward my face, and I'd get a shot at it. The Lakers were clearing out a side for him, and I had to discipline myself now, play good position and not reach out and try to take the ball away. If he went up, I'd go up straight right with him. Don't lean, I ordered myself. In my anxiousness, though, I went for the steal a few times and got called for the fouls. When I guarded West, I think sometimes I got the shaft because he was already a superstar and I was just an up-and-coming player then. The refs always give the big guys the benefit of the calls. Sometimes West would trip over his own feet and they'd call the foul on me.

With both Barnett and me in foul trouble, West got 16

by himself in the third period, and put the Lakers in front by 3. We knew what had to bring us back: defense, the way it had all year. In the fourth quarter, we doubled up more on West and got a few steals, and a few from Garrett when he brought the ball upcourt. The bench came in. Riordan and Cazzie ran the Lakers up and down the court, and with Wilt moving so slowly, there was no way the Lakers could stay with us. They even challenged Wilt on tough drives to the basket. The big man didn't get off the ground quick enough to block them. Willis got 37, Riordan got 19, and Cazzie scored 8 straight in the final quarter.

We won game one, 124–112.

On the off-day before game two of the series, I took Dickie Garrett around with me and showed him a few of the places along First Avenue and up in Harlem where I hang out. We both made a point of not talking at all about the game. I figured, though, that I had Garrett hooked on a sucker bet. No way the Lakers could beat us with Wilt moving the way he was in game one. If he wasn't going to come out on defense, I could deliver the ball all over the court, find the open man so much more easily. We were an outside shooting team, and if you didn't play us straight up, one of us was bound to get hot and do it.

I guess the Lakers had figured out the same thing. The first time we got the ball in game two, Willis went up to shoot a jumper near the foul line, and there was Wilt going out for him and putting a hand in his face. He didn't go out with him all the time, but enough so that Willis missed seventeen shots and the Lakers stayed right even with us through most of the game. With a minute to go, the score was tied again, at 103 apiece, just like it had been at the half and at the three-quarter mark. Riordan fouled West, who made both free throws. With twenty-two seconds to go, Barnett got the ball into Willis, who whirled around and tried to go up with a lay-up. As if he had been saving it up, Wilt got off his feet quicker this time, and cleanly blocked the shot. I got the ball back and over to DeBusschere, but he missed off the rim. The Rave came down with the rebound this time but then got called for a three-second violation. Jeezus, three shots at it and we still couldn't do it. Time ran out and the Lakers had accomplished what they came to New York to do: They had tied the series, and we had lost our home-court advantage. Maybe this wasn't going to be as easy as I had thought.

The Knicks management chartered a plane to take us out to the West Coast. It was just the players, Red and Danny, the reporters and photographers covering the team, Ned Irish, the team president, and his wife, on a 747. Everybody was loose, and if we were worried about losing the home-court advantage, nobody acted like it. There were two movies playing: one in first class, and one back where economy class would have been. I watched the movie in the front till I got a little bored, then moved to the back to watch the other film. Barnett and Phil Jackson, who although he was out for the year with his back injury was traveling with the team as a celebrity photographer, were having a big-money card game with some of the reporters up front. Everybody was laughing and joking, and I couldn't tell who was losing. The food—fish and chicken and shrimp—kept coming, and so did the booze. A number of the guys were just weaving through the aisles, more than a little inebriated by the time we reached California.

The L.A. crowd was pretty quiet, at least compared to what the Garden was like. I don't usually hear crowds much anyway, but even if I did, I wouldn't have heard them in the Forum. The seats are set way back from the court, and the fans weren't like New York fans. The crowd in New York knew its basketball. They knew when the team was playing well—not just when we were winning. They knew give-and-gos and backdoor plays and that defense is just as important as offense. The L.A. crowd cheered when there was a flashy play, when Baylor made a good move to the hoop, or West banged in a jumper under pressure. It it wasn't a sharp move, they didn't care. The L.A. fans also usually left the game early, even if it was tight. Gotta beat the traffic home, you know. Can't take the subway.

Behind West and Keith Erickson, the Lakers got off fast in game three and opened up a 14-point first-half lead. Then it was our turn to make a move on them and come back. DeBusschere started hitting, and Barnett got red-hot and scored 9 in a row. We tied it up in the fourth quarter at 96 all, with less than two minutes to go. It stayed tied until DeBusschere, out behind the foul line, put in a jumper. The score was Knicks 102, Lakers 100. With three seconds to go, I figured we had it.

Wilt took the ball out of bounds, except he never got out of bounds completely. He straddled the line, but no one saw it. The refs weren't looking at his feet, and neither were we. He threw the ball to West on the left side of the lane. I was at half court, and I was watching West closely. I could see his eyes. He took a few dribbles toward me, and there was real fire in those eyes.

He had momentum toward the basket, jumped, and, maybe sixty feet from the hoop, sent the ball flying. I didn't follow the shot, I didn't see the ball's trajectory. I just kept watching Jerry as I turned slightly to head off the court. Suddenly, there was a sort of buzz in the crowd, a sense, maybe, of anticipation. I turned around to look at the basket, and just as I did, I saw the damn ball go cleanly in. DeBusschere, who was under the basket, fell down, like his legs had gotten weak and just gone out from under him. "Damn," I said to myself, "Damn, damn, damn."

After watching the shot go in, Wilt left the court and headed toward the Lakers' locker room. He thought the game was over, and that L.A. had won it on the shot. I was still standing on the court and didn't know what to think. My mind was blank. Red called me over to the bench, but I didn't hear him. I felt drained, like I just woke up in the middle of the night and the middle of a nightmare. Finally, Red called me again; I heard him and I went like a robot over to the sideline. He was pretty composed. "Come on, we got to play, the game ain't over. We got to go five more minutes."

"God," I said to myself, "if we're supposed to win this game, you woulda never let that shot go in."

We were all still standing there a little bewildered while Red kept saying, "Hey, we got to play. We still can win this game." I was real skeptical of that. It didn't seem like we were meant to win it.

The Lakers found Wilt and got him back on the court, and we started the overtime. I remember almost nothing about it. I was still shell-shocked, I guess. I don't know how we did it, but we did it. West finally missed a few shots and Barnett hit a fall-back baby to put us ahead for good. We won the game 111–108 to go up 2–1 in the series.

The next night, as promised, Garrett showed me around L.A., like I had done for him in New York. Even though we tried not to talk about the games, I still felt awkward hanging out with him. Each time he wanted to show me a place, we had to drive about an hour to get to it. L.A. wasn't my kind of city.

We should've killed them in game four. We had come back from the dead to win despite West's shot. We had been kicked in the chest and still got up. It had been a tremendous ego boost. Our confidence was as high as it could be. And according to what I read in the paper, West might not even play in the next game because he had jammed his thumb. I didn't believe that for a second. West would get his nose broken every couple of weeks, and he always played. If a broken nose didn't stop him, I didn't think a jammed thumb would.

West played, of course. He started hitting the jumper early, and so we doubled up on him. He began passing the ball off, and the other Lakers were taking advantage of it. And for the first time in the series, we were really getting hurt by Elgin Baylor. Elgin had been one of the all-time greats, a terrific ballplayer to watch whether you were playing with him or against him. He had all the moves. He could jump, he could rebound, he could pass the ball, and he had a decent outside shot. When I came into the league as a rookie, he was still very tough. I remember after one game at the Garden, I was in the parking lot and saw him on the street. I was in total awe of him: I just stood and stared as he walked up the street toward his hotel. He had a snazzy, bopping kind of walk, sort of the way he played: He bounced, moving a shoulder here and giving a head fake there. "Wow," I said out loud, "that's Elgin."

It was obvious now that he was on the downside of his career. He couldn't play as long as he used to, and he was no longer an important part of the Laker offense. They didn't have a lot of plays running through him, and he had to get the points on his own now. And at this stage of his career, he was no longer the type of player who could do that all the time. Elgin had to operate down low to get his points, and Wilt wouldn't allow him to. Wilt wouldn't move from the low post, and there was no room for anyone else there. With three superstars on the Lakers, Elgin had become the odd man out. I felt a little sorry for him. The word around the league was that it was not a happy place, the L.A. locker room.

Still, Elgin wasn't completely through yet, and he proved it in game four. With moves that were like Doctor J's before there was a Doctor J, he got 30 points and 13 rebounds. West, too, had an okay game: 37 points and 18 assists. Still, we had a chance to win it in regulation, but with Erickson tight on me, I missed a jumper. It wasn't a great game for me or for the Knicks, and the Lakers took it in overtime to tie the series at 2 games all. There was only one consolation: We were going home.

Before game five, Danny and Red had another problem.

Willis was starting to favor his knees more than usual. He never talked much about pain, not when he broke his nose or anything else. Now, though, he was starting to say how bad the knees felt. I saw him in Danny's room getting a cortisone shot and soaking his knees in the whirlpool. "Hey, how you feelin'?" I asked him. "It's hurting a little," he said. I didn't know what that meant exactly. There was no way to tell how much pain he was really feeling. There was no way to know how long he could keep going.

He went for about nine minutes more, and it wasn't even his knees that did it. With 3:56 left in the first quarter of game five, Willis took a pass from DeBusschere and tried to drive around Wilt. As he headed for the hoop, he tripped over Wilt's foot and landed heavily on his right hip. The moment is frozen in my mind as if it happened yesterday. Willis is lying on the floor with a horrible look of pain on his face. The refs don't call a time-out. They don't do anything. Don't they see him? Wilt picks the ball and throws it down to the other end, where all the action goes. Red is screaming, "You *jerks,* stop the game. Stop the game. A man is hurt." Willis tries to get up and follow the ball downcourt, but he can barely move. DeBusschere ties Wilt up, and finally the refs give us a time-out.

We all moved over to form a circle around Willis, but Red didn't let us huddle like that for very long. "Hey," he said, "the game's still got to go on. Come on." I love that about Red. No one man is the show; the game is the thing. I'm sure he was concerned, but, hey, we couldn't just stop the game and go home. Danny and the team doctor walked Willis off the court and into the locker room. There goes the championship, I thought. That's it. No way. I remembered the sucker bet I had made with Dickie Garrett. I guessed I was the sucker now.

Even before Willis went down, Wilt, who was more aggressive than he had been in the first four games, already had scored 11 points and was looking to go to the basket on almost every possession. Who was going to stop him now? It looked pretty plain that Willis wouldn't be coming back, at least for the rest of the first half. Nate Bowman came off the bench to replace him, with the Lakers already up by 10. For the first couple of minutes with Nate in there, both teams played sloppy ball. Then the Butcher hit a pair of jumpers and the Lakers, surprisingly, called a time-out. Why? Could they be a little nervous? The first quarter ended with us still 10 behind, but that was no worse than what we had been before Willis went down.

Cazzie came in for the second period and got us some points, but the Lakers were now starting to look for Wilt, and he was beginning to put it to Nate. The Lakers raised their lead to 13 when Red called a time-out. He took Bowman out of the game and put in Bill Hosket. Hosket is only around 6′ 7″, but, after Willis and Nate, he was the biggest guy we had. Hosket had not played a minute in the play-offs. He hadn't seen any action against Baltimore, Milwaukee, or in the first four L.A. games. The only times Hosket ever got to play during the season was when the game was a total blowout. He probably shouldn't even have been on the team. Now he was going up against Wilt Chamberlain, basketball's greatest scorer, in the most important game we had played all year. I mean, the situation looked ridiculous for us.

This was the time we could've said, Hey, man, you guys got this one. We'll take our chances in the next game. Let's fold our tents and wait for tomorrow. There are times players do that. They're not tanking it, they're just mentally saving themselves for the next game. Still, we didn't shake hands and walk off. If you stay on the court, you never know what can happen.

Hosket, running around and waving his arms, held Wilt without a point for the next several minutes while the Lakers started to make some mistakes, nervous mistakes. Mel Counts was called for walking, and then John Tresvant walked. Wilt, as always, missed some foul shots, even though he had been hitting them before. Cazzie continued to score. With a little more than four minutes to go in the half, Red took out Hosket and put in the Butcher to go up against Wilt. Dave is so much smaller than Chamberlain, I didn't think Wilt could even see him. Dave ran him back and forth, trying to stay under him, and between Wilt and the ball. When Wilt brought the ball down, Dave—and the rest of us, too—tried to snipe at him, to flick the ball away, or at least to slow down an outlet pass. The Lakers kept trying to get the ball into him, and that was starting to get their game out of sync. They wanted desperately to utilize their height advantage, rather than just letting it happen spontaneously. Wilt didn't score any more in the first half, and we went into the locker room still trailing by only 13.

Willis was lying on the table in Danny's room. The doctor was with him, and told Red—who told us—that Willis had a severely strained tensor muscle, whatever that is, high in the right thigh. He was not going to be playing anymore tonight. I couldn't tell a thing from Red's face or voice or the way he was acting if he was worried or didn't care or what. Nothing ever changed with him. He was very businesslike as he went over what we had to do defensively in the second half to get back in the game. Help out on Wilt. Try to force him to the baseline. Look to double him whenever he got the ball. If Wilt passed it out and West or Baylor or Erickson beat us, okay. But let's see if they can. Then Red turned to offense and did something he almost never did. He asked for suggestions.

Dollar Bill had one. How about, he says, trying a 1-3-1 offense, with Barnett and Cazzie at the wings, me at the top of the key, Bradley himself around the foul line, and DeBusschere under the basket running the baseline? It's the

kind of offense you try in high school, when you're playing a better, taller team that's using a zone. It's supposed to force them to come out and away from the basket, which is what we wanted to do with Wilt. If he does move to cover the corners or DeBusschere, we open up the lane for drives and offensive rebounds. If he doesn't come out, then in theory one of us should have an open shot. I didn't know if the strategy would work. It seemed to me that it was a real long shot, but we needed something, anything. We had to try a different way to play and see if we could score some points. This was better than anything else we had. And if it didn't work, we could always can it. Hey, we were losing anyway, right?

As we got ready to go back on the court, we patted one another enthusiastically on the backs. With Willis out, there was a lot more emotion than usual. It was like we were trying to make up for his absence by talking louder and pumping our arms more. "We can do it!" Bradley shouted. "If we play good defense, we can do it." The next day in the papers, I read that right before we went out, Red had told us to "Win this one for the captain." It didn't happen. That wasn't the way Red worked. Barnett said it—"Hey, men, we gotta win this thing for Captain Willis"—but he was being facetious and we all laughed.

It looked like David and Goliath as DeBusschere took the center jump against Chamberlain to begin the second half. We started off in the 1-3-1, and it was working. Wilt didn

move out, and Cazzie was able to score from close in, and then DeBusschere and Bradley were able to get pretty open shots and hit them. Meanwhile, the Lakers were concentrating only on getting the ball into Wilt, and the rest of them were just standing around. On paper, at least, it was the ideal strategy: Reed is out, so let's go inside. But they kept forcing passes into Wilt and we kept picking them off. When they did get it into him, we were swarming all over and he couldn't get the ball back to West or the other Lakers. They were not taking advantage of the double teaming. They were not finishing us off, the way they should have been doing, and that gave us confidence. I was starting to think that not only could we put up a good fight, we could win this damn thing. We had a real chance at beating these guys. Yes.

The Lakers were losing their poise. They had already lost their continuity and their momentum. At the end of the quarter, we had cut their lead to 7. Man, we believe.

In the first few minutes of the final quarter, we got the lead down to 3. And then the Butcher gets his fifth foul. Who can we play now? Red brought in the Rave to go against Wilt, who probably outweighed him by eighty or ninety pounds. Still, the first time Stalls touched the ball, he hit a jumper from the sideline. The next time we got possession, Barnett scored again and the Los Angeles lead was one.

The crowd was going absolutely out of its mind. The fans were shouting, "Dee-fense, DEE-fense," like they'd never

shouted it before. The Lakers were in trouble. When you're on the road, you've got to keep the crowd out of the game. Once you let the fans get involved, you're letting the home players get psyched. They'll reach a different level then, a higher, more confident level. The visiting team becomes more doubtful about what they're doing. They can't hear themselves think. They're confused and start to think the game out rather than just reacting to the flow.

During a time-out, when we were usually so quiet and unemotional, we were now pumping each other up and saying, "Let's go, let's go. We got 'em, we got 'em." West made a free throw to put them up by 2, then with 7:43 to go in the game, Dollar got a pass from Cazzie and put in a jumper to tie the score at 87. The crowd went completely berserk. The roar was so loud it almost hurt my ears. People were stomping their feet, and I thought the top level of the Garden was going to start shaking and then crash down right on top of us.

Two minutes later, Bradley got the ball near the top of the key again, with the seven-footer Mel Counts on him. Counts is around seven inches taller than Dollar, and I was sure he was going to block the shot, bounce it off the scoreboard. Bradley just got it over his fingertips and the ball went in. We had our first lead of the night.

I didn't think it could happen, but the roar got even louder. I was so excited I had goose bumps. 'Course, I thought, if you ain't excited in a game like this, man, you don't have a pulse at all. You are stone-cold dead. The Lakers looked tentative and disoriented. They didn't know what to do with the ball. Their coach, Joe Mullaney, was up in front of their bench screaming at them to run their plays, run their plays, but they weren't listening to anybody.

We had it now. We knew we had it.

The Lakers kept turning the ball over. The Rave and Dollar and Cazzie kept scoring. Finally, Wilt came out one time to guard Stalls. The Rave gave him one of his herky-jerky moves, drove right past Wilt and under the hoop for a reverse lay-up. The crowd was now completely on its feet. I felt that we were an extension of the crowd, we were floating away on their cheers. The game was becoming comical. I wanted to laugh, the whole thing was so ridiculous, but I had to keep my game face on. We won going away, 107–100.

Everybody said was it Wilt's fault. Chamberlain should have scored 100 against us. He should have wiped up the court with Bowman and Hosket and DeBusschere and Stallworth. He should've gone to the hoop more or should've passed more. He should've won the game for the Lakers and he didn't. He had lost another one, another big one.

The press always blamed Wilt because a lot of writers didn't like him. He was an arrogant man, and he was not always cordial to the press—or to anybody else. Everybody knew he was a moody kind of guy. Some days he might speak to you and other days he might look right through you. It all depended on which side of bed he got up on that morning. I didn't know him well, but at one time he was friends with a girl I was dating. I'd go past him at the free-throw line and he'd say, in that extremely deep voice, "Hi, Walt, how's Sophia doing?" The next game we played against him, he'd just walk by me all night without saying a word.

He might've had some reasons for being moody. When he first came into the league, all the tough guys tried to kick his butt. It was a real prejudiced league back then, and he was one of the first important black players. I'm sure a lot of the white guys wanted to test him, see how tough he was. He was making big money, and there was also a lot of jealousy directed at him. The players were extremely physical, and he was Wilt the Stilt then, just a tall, skinny guy—not the massive he-man he turned into later. He got roughed up so much in those early years, I'd heard that he'd thought of leaving the league.

As the biggest guy, he was naturally always the villain. It was easy to pick on him. When he led the league in scoring, everybody said he couldn't pass off. So he led the league in assists, and people started to complain that he couldn't score anymore. He got the reputation of not being a clutch ballplayer, not being a winner, and I thought that was unfair. Sure, Bill Russell won more than he did, but Russell always had better teams around him than Wilt did. Wilt was a pressure player. I have to believe that when you have the stats he had, you *have* to be a pressure player. When the game was on the line, I felt Wilt would do something to win. He'd block your shot, or get that key rebound, or slam down the dunk. Like West or John Havlicek or a few others, he was a player who could beat us single-handed, I used to feel.

Even though he's now over fifty years old, I think Wilt could still play in the league. Really. Because there's no defense in today's game, he could still be a factor, just by his size and strength and presence, and just playing defense. Wilt's not going to run up and down the court much, and he wouldn't have to worry about getting back and setting up on offense. He couldn't, probably even if he tried, do much offensively, so he would just play the one end of the court. But he could be used as a situational defense player, with the coach putting him in according to what the strategy at that time demanded. With his body and long reach, he could still intimidate guys and get his team maybe ten rebounds a game, and maybe even dominate some games.

He could do it because the big men today just aren't that good. If Kareem, as great as he has been, can still play acceptably past the age of forty, I think it's sufficient proof of the quality of the league's big men. Sure, Wilt might have trouble with players like Akeem Olajuwon and Robert Parrish and Moses Malone, but he probably wouldn't handle them any worse than their opponents do today. And Wilt could be stronger than those guys and really push them around, and make them work for everything. With the exceptions of Akeem, Patrick Ewing, and a few others, the big men today are all one-dimensional, just like Wilt would be if he came back. They can only do one thing, either shoot or rebound, not both. Alton Lister makes a million dollars a year, and what kind of shot does he have? And is he more intimidating today than Wilt would be?

There are a lot more big men today, two or three seven-footers on each team, but most of them have height, and that's it. I guess that's always been the case, a few really good big men and the rest just filling up space. Today, though, most of the seven-footers don't seem to come within ten feet of the basket. Part of it is that they widened the lane about fifteen years ago, and that meant the centers had to set up further from the hoop. But guys like Bill Laimbeer and Jack Sikma play the game like guards. They don't want to go under the basket and take advantage of their height. How can you have a man 6' 10" or better who doesn't have an inside game? What did their coaches teach these guys? Come to think of it, maybe Bill Russell could also come back as a player and be a factor.

When I was growing up, I always liked Wilt. He was one of my idols. I thought he was a handsome guy, a cool dude, and a great player. He dominated the game as maybe no one else ever has, and became the greatest offensive weapon in the history of the game. Yeah, he really wasn't a team player, but I don't know if that was all his fault. Ballplayers are the extension of their coaches. If Wilt had played for coaches who had disciplined him and made him into a complete player, he would have been not just one of the greatest, but the greatest player ever, no question. If he had had the coaching I did, he would have been unbelievable.

When Wilt missed free throws in game five, the fans booed the hell out of him. They always liked to boo Wilt. I had no sympathy at all. He had already been to the mountaintop. I hadn't.

After the win in game five, we went into the locker room and immediately we all started asking about Willis. How bad was he? Could he play in game six? What was his status right now? Willis was still there, in his street clothes by now. He was limping pretty bad, and there wasn't much reason to think he'd be able to go the next time out. "A day-to-day thing," he told some of the guys. "It's a little better than it was before, but hey, man, I just don't know."

For the next couple of days, the newspapers, TV, and radio speculated about whether he'd play. I knew he wouldn't. He didn't have to. It didn't matter if we didn't have him and lost game six. There would still be one more to play, and it would be in New York. There'd still be some light left in the tunnel.

Willis was not going to play. Before we went out on the court for number six, Red announced to us that Bowman would be the starter. "Man," Barnett said as we headed out, "you sure better get a hearse out there. Ain't no way that sucker is gonna make it through the whole game."

When the Lakers came out for the introductions, the fans, the *home* crowd, booed them. It was like going back to your own house and your mother has your suitcase waiting on the steps before she kicks you out. Red threw Nate and Stalls and Hosket and DeBusschere against Wilt and none of them made any difference this time. We'd lost the element of surprise. The Lakers had had time to regroup and figure out how to run their plays and attack us. Wilt got 45 points and 27 rebounds and passed off when he should for easy baskets by West and Dickie Garrett. We were never in it at all. There was going to be a game seven.

We had been blown out, yet I still figured we had a shot, a small one, to win one more game this season. We could come back. We had done it in game five and proved that it could be done. All we needed was Willis, just a little bit of him, just enough of him.

On Friday, the day of the final game, I left the New Yorker and went to the Garden for a ten o'clock meeting and shoot-around. Willis wasn't there, and everybody was reading the papers and trying to get the latest information on his condition. What do *you* know, we all asked one another, and it seemed that no one knew very much.

When I got back to the Garden in the early evening after my lazy day of conserving energy, Willis was in uniform, in Danny's room, after getting a final shot of cortisone and another shot of a painkiller. He had the ultrasound machine, which looks sort of like a telephone, pressed against his thigh. He had worked out a half hour or so before, testing the leg, and there was still sweat on his face. He hoped the painkiller would help, and thought it would. But with the game only a few minutes off, he still didn't know, he told me, if he'd be able to go.

Before we walked out to the floor, Bradley spoke quietly to Willis and asked him to "just give us a half. That's all we need." He was right. Half of Willis Reed was more than 100 percent of anybody else we could put out there on the court.

We went out to warm up and Willis didn't come with us. We left him in the locker room, and I figured that if he could play, he would be with us now. If he could play, he would. If there was any possibility at all, Willis would be there.

The fans in the rows nearest the court shouted out to us, "Hey, is Willis going to play?" "How's Willis's leg? Can he jump enough to play?" After a few minutes on the floor, Barnett said to me, "We gotta forget about Reed. Man, we have to play it anyway, even if he doesn't play. We're the team now. It's us who gotta do it."

At 7:27 exactly, just a few minutes before game time, I heard a rumbling roar, like a thunderstorm moving slowly through a valley. The only other time I've heard a sound like that was at one game when a girl with tremendous breasts walked through the crowd and everyone stood up in turn to get a look and give her a standing ovation. When I heard it again this time, I turned to look at the commotion, figuring that some movie star had come in and the fans were recognizing him. Or maybe the same girl had come back. I didn't look at the tunnel that leads from the locker rooms, but up in the stands to see which star was getting such a reaction. Then, all of a sudden, everyone in the whole place was on their feet, applauding and shouting and I saw Willis. So did the Lakers. Willis warmed up a little, took a few shots, and I saw that the Lakers were absolutely mesmerized. They'd completely stopped what they were doing and were just watching Willis get warm. They were not cool about it. If they wanted to watch, they should've done it discreetly. They should have acted like they didn't care what in hell Reed was doing. Yeah, bring Reed on, man, we'll kick your butts anyway.

Willis was moving mechanically. He was not dragging his leg too much, but it was obvious he was not the fluid, normal Willis Reed. It didn't matter. The fans were cheering every move he made. If he'd tied his shoelaces, they'd have cheered that, too. I was cool. I had my deadpan on, just like

I'd been doing since high school. But in my heart, I felt like cheering, too.

When we went out for the introductions of the players, I could feel my heart beating. Bradley and DeBusschere used to say that when they were lining up, they picked out a face—say, a pretty lady in the third row behind the bench—and they'd concentrate on her. Even if I tried, I couldn't see a single face now. They'd all blurred together. The organist didn't get halfway through the national anthem before the noise of the crowd overwhelmed his music. With the exception of a hockey play-off game I once went to, this was definitely the loudest crowd I'd ever heard.

The ref threw the ball up for the opening tap, and Willis didn't jump for it. We got the ball back almost immediately, and I hit Willis with a pass. He was out near the foul line, completely alone. What kind of strategy was this for the Lakers? They had to know that Willis couldn't drive around anyone, and Chamberlain just stood back in the lane and was going to let him shoot from the outside. Willis couldn't move, and still Wilt wouldn't get up on him. Willis jumped as best he could and shot that soft jump shot. It touched nothing but net. Unbelievable.

He ain't hurt, I thought. I knew he was, he had to be, but I could push it out of my mind now. I could believe that the real Willis Reed was out there with us on the court.

A few seconds later, Willis got the ball about twenty feet

out and scored again. I was so turned on, I thought I was going to jump out of the Garden. I think I ran down the floor with a smile on my face. Willis didn't score another point the rest of the night. He didn't even get many rebounds for us. For most of the time he stayed in there, we used him to set picks and screens and to get between Wilt and the boards. We didn't need him for anything else. He'd turned us all on.

I felt as pumped up as I ever have on a basketball court. I wanted to take charge of the game, dominate every second of it. I wanted to give Willis back what he'd done for us. With my friend Dickie Garrett guarding me, I hit five shots in a row in the first quarter. Each time down, I wanted the ball. For almost six weeks of play-offs, I hadn't scored very much. I'd been concentrating on defense and on moving the ball around. Now, it was time for me to do some scoring. For one of the few times in my career, I was actively looking for my shots. I wasn't just waiting to be the open man.

When there was a time-out, the guys on the bench were all standing up for us, waiting for us to come to the sideline. In the huddle, there was more enthusiasm than I'd ever seen with the Knicks. We were cheering and encouraging one another and clapping without stopping. I was encouraged, yet I was still scared. How much longer could we play this well? When was the lull going to come? Halfway through the second quarter, I stole the ball from West, and then Riordan forced Jerry into a twenty-four-second violation on their next possession. West looked bewildered. For that one moment, he was out of control, and you never saw that happen with Jerry. We'd wounded their leader. I knew we had them now.

In the locker room at halftime, no one could sit down. Cazzie and the Rave were literally jumping up and down. Everybody was saying, "All right, all *right.*" We couldn't stop slapping one another's hands.

The P.A. announcer said that Nate Bowman would be starting at center for the Knicks in the second half. No way. Just before Nate stepped into the circle, Willis walked out and replaced him. Wilt had a "what-the-hell-is-going-on-here" look on his face. It was like the whole evening was choreographed. Willis played only a few more minutes, without scoring another point. Meanwhile, I scored 36, handed out 19 assists, and made about 5 or 6 steals, in what I think was the best game I've ever played, considering the circumstances. No one even much noticed it, though, because there was too much else going on. There was too much else to think about and write about. The next day, and for a few days after, that would bother me a little. Tonight, though, nothing at all could disturb me. The final score was New York 113, Los Angeles 99. The Knicks were champions of the world.

CHAPTER

10

ON THE NIGHT OF MAY 8, 1970, I DIDN'T WANT TO
be cool anymore. I can finally relax, I thought, and let
it all hang out. Of course, letting it all hang out for me is
being cool for most people. Still, I figured that at last I could
have me a real good time with no worries about tomorrow.
I didn't understand at first what it meant to be world
champs, and how it would affect my life. I didn't think much
about prestige and records and money. No, man, at first I
saw it in terms of parties. I was going to make as many of
them as I could.

My man Sweet, who was my driver, took me everywhere
that night, East Side, West Side, uptown, downtown. No
matter where I went, I couldn't buy a drink for myself. No
one would let me. It was champagne everywhere, Dom Per-
ignon mixed with orange juice, and I said to hell with my
self-imposed limit, I don't have to drive tonight. I met a lot
of ladies throughout the evening, but I didn't want to take
any of them home this night. I just wanted to have fun and

stay out forever. Sometime near dawn, I ran into Nate and the Rave up at Small's Paradise. I think they were as far gone as I was. I got in somewhere around six or seven in the morning and threw myself on the bed without getting undressed. When I finally woke up, I had missed a reception for the team given by the mayor of New York. I was really hung over. I felt great.

A few months after the season ended, I collected on my bet. I went back to Carbondale, where Dickie Garrett threw a very nice party in my honor.

Three years after the Knicks won the title, we won another one, also against the Lakers. The funny thing is, I can barely remember that second championship. I know we did it, because people have told me we did and because I have a championship ring from that year. I guess Earl was with me that time instead of against me and Jerry Lucas was there instead of Cazzie Russell and he and Willis shared the middle. Yet I can hardly recall the specific details of the championship, how I played, what we did to win, who played well. The 1973 title was just basketball, nothing more.

Even if I wanted to, I couldn't forget the first championship. No one will let me. Almost twenty years later, I can't walk the streets of New York without people bringing it up to me. I'll be jogging in Central Park and somebody will shout out, "Hey, Clyde, great game against the Lakers." They still remember Willis limping and making those first two shots and the winning streak and me against the Pearl. The rest is a happy blur. I still meet people all the time who tell me, "I never watched a sport, and never really cared much about basketball, until I saw you guys play. And I haven't watched it since."

The 1970 Knicks still live. More than any club I've ever heard of, that team was a part of people's lives. In the beginning, I thought it was just the guys on the team who cared, and then the fans who followed us closely. But we touched people from all over, and it's a memory that remains in their minds, and that will remain forever. At first I thought it was because it was the first championship ever for the Knicks that made it significant. But it was really the way we won. It was the circumstances and the style that were unforgettable. Just winning it wouldn't have been enough. There was a feeling of destiny about it all. The win that broke the record, the play-offs, Willis's injury, the final game. I've always believed that if the Lakers had played us one hundred times in game seven, they would have beaten us ninety-nine times. The one time it counted, though, they didn't. Throughout the year, everything fell into place. When I had a chance to think about it, I realized that was the only way it could have happened.

The Knicks were a class act, and I think people realized that. We were players who could be respected, men who took care of their private lives and put something back into the community. We were intelligent players and also intelligent people, who generally could speak well and come off like we knew what we were talking about. We had it all—glamour, intelligence, true grit. The NBA was just starting to come into focus as a major sport, and we helped create that and then took advantage of it.

After we won, I thought we would do it every year. It didn't really dawn on me until years later, after I had left the game, that we had done something very special.

I've been out of basketball for ten years now. At first I missed the traveling and the camaraderie and the challenge of being a hero every other night. For about two years after I retired, I could not watch a professional basketball game. It could have been that I had had too much of it, or that I was bitter my time had passed. All I knew was that I preferred football on TV.

When I left the NBA, I didn't leave wealthy. The Cavaliers had to pay me for the final year of my contract, and I suppose I was financially secure, but it all depended on how I wanted to live, how free and easy I wanted to be.

I was more concerned about what I would do and how I'd occupy my time. At first there was a void in my life. I felt sometimes that I should be someplace and I was no longer there. A lot of times I thought, Shouldn't I be practicing now? I needed a new challenge in my life, and I had to create one for myself. I decided that my challenge would be becoming as successful in business as I had been in sports.

At first with my old partner Irwin Weiner, and then by myself, I tried being a sports agent. That gave me the opportunity to go on the road, which I missed, and to be with players, which I missed, too. I concentrated on football players—you have a lot more bodies than in basketball—and found that driving with a friend through Alabama, Mississippi, and Louisiana, on the lookout for talent, was the next best thing to playing. Although I never had any real big-name players, I was doing pretty well at it for a few years until I got tired of baby-sitting college athletes to make sure no other agents would steal them away. Nobody baby-sat me when I was in college.

After my playing career ended, I thought some about coaching, but it seemed too much like hard work. I didn't want to devote twelve months a year to *anything*. I could coach kids—I still run a basketball camp, which gives me a lot more pleasure than money—but not players who already think they know all it takes.

I was back home in Atlanta while my agent business ran its course, when I got an offer to come back to New York, to be a host at a fancy sports bar for Wall Street types. The hours, smoke, and noise of the club eventually got to be too much, but it was a good opportunity to get back to Manhattan. Now I'm a vice-president of sales for a business-service company, and I do commercials and different kinds of public appearances. I also find I can watch pro basketball games again and do color commentary for Knick broadcasts.

For the last few years, I've also been going into the New York City public schools and giving speeches. A lot of the kids don't know me—hell, they were five when I retired—but that doesn't matter, because I have something to say. I talk to them about discipline, about making something of themselves, about how they have to listen and not think they know everything there is to know. I talk to them about drugs and alcohol, too.

Drugs really weren't much of a problem when I played. Alcohol was the most prevalent drug around, particularly among the older players. It was only in the late sixties that some of the younger players started bringing pot into the game.

I talk to the kids because I feel a responsibility to give something back. And maybe, too, it's because two of my sisters died from drugs. I can vividly remember exactly when I heard about my sister Janice. It was the day of a game, and I had just finished running the stairs, when I got the call at home from my mother. When she told me my sister had died from heroin, I assumed she was talking about Brenda, the third oldest, who had always lived wild and fast. Only at the end of the conversation did my mother say Janice's name. She had been a tomboy. No one had ever told me she was into drugs. A couple of years later, Brenda, too, died of an overdose of heroin. All of us in the family said she didn't really want to live.

Though I'm glad to be back in New York, I don't spend all my time there. In St. Croix, the Virgin Islands, I have a house and a boat, a trimaran. I went down there for the first time almost ten years ago, on a vacation with my son, and I was hooked. I had never slept so well in my life. I wanted to buy a condo and ended up with the house and then the boat, and then earning my captain's license. Passing the license test was as tough as guarding Oscar or Earl. One of these days, I'm going to start a chartering service down there, Sail Away with Captain Clyde. Sailing gives me great pleasure, and I love it. I suppose, though, that I'll never love anything as much as I loved basketball.

A lot of my old Knick teammates used to think that of all of us, I would probably have the hardest time adjusting to life after basketball. Because of my vanity, because Barnett sometimes used to call me "Max Factor," they thought I wouldn't be able to live outside the limelight. I think, though, that I've adjusted better than most of the guys. I'm at peace with myself today, more than I ever was.

I'm more Walt now, with Clyde only coming out occasionally. Sometimes I miss him. I had a good time as Clyde. I liked meeting people and talking more than I realized. But I don't seek that anymore. Clyde is only a part-time player today, mainly because I don't go out nearly as often. I realize that I'm a retired player. In my own mind, I'm no longer a star.

I'm not really much in touch these days with the guys from the team. Our relationships were basically professional, not social. The Rave, I've heard, has a regular job back home in Wichita. Willis is coaching the Nets, and Cazzie is an assistant coach with the Atlanta Hawks. DeBusschere is doing something on Wall Street. Red is retired, living out on Long Island. Danny Whelan is semi-retired, but still works with some kids in the city. Nate Bowman, of course, died a few years ago from a heart atack. Johnny Warren is an accountant with one of the larger firms. Dollar Bill has some kind of job in Washington, I think. When and if he goes for the biggest job there, I'll support him. Barnett is living in New Jersey, and still wheeling and dealing in different ventures. I ran into Mike Riordan a couple of years ago, down in Annapolis, Maryland. I had gone there for a boat show, and one afternoon when I was looking to have lunch, I saw a crowded, jumping place named Riordan's. Someone had mentioned to me that he thought Mike owned a restaurant in the town, and I wondered. I walked in, and in the back, working just as hard as he had with the Knicks, was Mike, still not sitting down for a meal. Hosket and May are probably back home in Ohio. I'm the only one left in New York City.

For winning the title, each of the players got around eight thousand dollars, and the Knick management added a little on top of that. We also got championship rings. Some of the guys put their rings in trophy cases, but I love wearing mine. Every time I put it on, I feel proud. It reminds me that I did something many guys could only dream about.

Today, it's the league office itself that has the rings made up and then gives them out to the championship team. The Knicks, though, had their own rings made, and had them encrusted with a bed of diamonds. On the rings, they also engraved in clear letters just one simple word: "Defense."

STATISTICS

Eastern Division	W	L	Western Division	W	L
New York Knicks	60	22	Atlanta Hawks	48	34
Milwaukee Bucks	56	26	Los Angeles Lakers	46	36
Baltimore Bullets	50	32	Chicago Bulls	39	43
Philadelphia 76ers	42	40	Phoenix Suns	39	43
Cincinnati Royals	36	46	Seattle Supersonics	36	46
Boston Celtics	34	48	San Francisco Warriors	30	52
Detroit Pistons	31	51	San Diego Rockets	27	55

THE PLAY-OFFS

Eastern Division Semifinals

Knicks 120, Bullets 117 (two overtimes), at New York
Knicks 106, Bullets 99, at Baltimore
Bullets 127, Knicks 113, at New York
Bullets 102, Knicks 92, at Baltimore
Knicks 101, Bullets 80, at New York
Bullets 96, Knicks 87, at Baltimore
Knicks 127, Bullets 114, at New York
Knicks win series, four games to three.

Eastern Division Finals

Knicks 110, Bucks 102, at New York
Knicks 112, Bucks 111, at New York
Bucks 101, Knicks 96, at Milwaukee
Knicks 117, Bucks 105, at Milwaukee
Knicks 132, Bucks 96, at New York
Knicks win series, four games to one.

NBA Championship Series

Knicks 124, Lakers 112, at New York
Lakers 105, Knicks 103, at New York
Knicks 111, Lakers 108 (overtime), at Los Angeles
Lakers 121, Knicks 115 (overtime), at Los Angeles
Knicks 107, Lakers 100, at New York
Lakers 135, Knicks 113, at Los Angeles
Knicks 113, Lakers 99, at New York
Knicks win series and championship, four games to three.

1969–70 NEW YORK KNICKS

	Games	Pnts.	Reb.	A.	Avg.
Dick Barnett	82	1,220	221	298	14.9
Nate Bowman	81	237	257	46	2.9
Bill Bradley	67	971	239	268	14.5
Dave DeBusschere	79	1,152	790	194	14.6
Walt Frazier	77	1,609	465	629	20.9
Bill Hosket	36	118	63	17	3.3
Don May	37	96	52	17	2.6

1969-70 NEW YORK KNICKS

	Games	Pnts.	Reb.	A.	Avg.
Willis Reed	81	1,775	1,126	161	21.7
Mike Riordan	81	624	194	201	7.7
Cazzie Russell	78	894	236	135	11.5
Dave Stallworth	82	639	323	139	7.8
John Warren	44	112	40	30	2.5

WALT FRAZIER IN THE NBA

Team and year	Games	Pnts.	Reb.	A.	Avg.
New York, 1968	74	666	313	305	9.0
New York, 1969	80	1,403	499	635	17.5
New York, 1970	77	1,609	465	629	20.9
New York, 1971	80	1,736	544	536	21.7
New York, 1972	77	1,788	513	446	23.2
New York, 1973	78	1,648	570	461	21.1
New York, 1974	80	1,643	536	551	20.5
New York, 1975	78	1,675	465	474	21.5
New York, 1976	59	1,126	400	351	19.1
New York, 1977	76	1,323	293	403	17.4
Cleveland, 1978	51	825	209	209	16.2
Cleveland, 1979	12	129	20	32	10.9
Totals	822	15,571	4,827	5,032	18.9

KNICK RECORDS HELD BY WALT FRAZIER

Career: most games, points, assists, total minutes played, field goals attempted, field goals made, free throws attempted. Play-offs: most points, assists, minutes, field goals attempted, field goals made, free throws attempted, free throws made.

THE 18-GAME WINNING STREAK, OCTOBER 24–NOVEMBER 28, 1969

Oct. 24, Knicks 116, Pistons 92, at Detroit
Oct. 25, Knicks 128, Bullets 99, at Madison Square Garden
Oct. 28, Knicks 128, Hawks 104, at Madison Square Garden
Oct. 30, Knicks 123, Rockets 110, at Madison Square Garden
Nov. 1, Knicks 112, Bucks 108, at Madison Square Garden
Nov. 3, Knicks 109, Bucks 93, at Milwaukee
Nov. 4, Knicks 116, Suns 99, at Phoenix
Nov. 7, Knicks 129, Rockets 111, at San Diego
Nov. 9, Knicks 112, Lakers 102, at Los Angeles
Nov. 11, Knicks 116, Warriors 103, at San Francisco
Nov. 13, Knicks 114, Bulls 99, at Madison Square Garden
Nov. 15, Knicks 113, Celtics 98, at Madison Square Garden
Nov. 18, Knicks 112, Royals 94, at Madison Square Garden
Nov. 21, Knicks 98, Sixers 94, at Philadelphia
Nov. 22, Knicks 128, Suns 114, at Madison Square Garden
Nov. 25, Knicks 103, Lakers 96, at Madison Square Garden
Nov. 26, Knicks 138, Hawks 108, at Atlanta
Nov. 28, Knicks 106, Royals 105, at Cleveland
Nov. 29, Pistons 110, Knicks 98, at Madison Square Garden